I'd Rather Die Than Obey

I'd Rather Die Than Obey

Trusting God Even When It Hurts

Dawn Tolbert

Eila Impressions

I dedicate this book to parents,
Jimmy and Barbara Camp,
models of obedience and faithfulness.

Contents

Introduction

Ready for some fishing?

I followed Daddy to the edge of the pasture. He easily climbed through the barbed wire fence and turned to hold the lowest two strands apart for me. I concentrated on clearing the wires, first with one leg, then my body, and finally pulled the other leg through. I'd almost cleared this big hurdle when my straw hat—just like the one he wore, only tinier—caught on the wire and spilled onto a clump of weeds. With a giggle, I grabbed it, gave it a shake, and plopped it back on my head, nearly toppling myself in the process.

Up the small hill we went. I took huge steps trying to follow in Daddy's footprints. He gripped our fishing poles in one hand, using them to push away briers so his baby girl had a clear path. Finally, we found a grassy spot on the edge of the pond and settled between clumps of stubbly weeds. He skillfully managed our poles, reaching around the squirming little girl by his side. Long, slender fingers deftly guided bait on the hook; then he placed those hands over mine and cast the line into the water.

We leaned back to wait on a nibble.

I'd love to know what we talked about, or have concrete details beyond faded snapshots of us holding the fish we caught. I recall warm sun on our faces, and I can almost hear frogs splashing and flies buzzing. Most of all, I remember how safe I felt as I rested in the arms of my father and enjoyed the security of his presence.

I could just imagine the grand fish tales we would have to tell.

The memory of that afternoon of fishing has been a swirling eddy in my mind as I thought about writing on the book of Jonah. His story is a lot like my own.

God called him to a task, and he ran away. He didn't want to be part of God's plan because it meant good would come to people he didn't like.

My reasons are different, but I see myself reflected in Jonah.

Way too clearly.

Several years ago, I prayed and asked God to show me how he wanted to use my writing for his glory. I started a blog and challenged myself to write every day for a year. (Of course, it had to be leap year!) Through the process, I felt God calling me to point women to his love and his call for us to turn away from worrying so much about ourselves and to turn to him. I wanted to help us turn our eyes from what can feel like overwhelming circumstances to focus on the One who calms the storm and his children. I knew I was called to encourage women—and myself—to let our lights shine for God in this dark world. This assignment felt like an incredibly scary thing to do.

It's still scary.

---

*My light can easily grow dim under stress and worry when
I give in to my own striving and take my eyes off Jesus.*

I'm far from perfect. I've made my share of mistakes and then
some. I have sinned willfully. My light can easily grow dim under
stress and worry when I give in to my own striving and take my eyes
off Jesus.

I found myself wondering how God could possibly use someone
whose heart so easily chases after its own dreams and desires. Then
I remembered David in the Bible, who was a shepherd boy turned
psalmist turned king. He was careful to remind his own heart to
remember the goodness of God. In Psalm 103:2, he wrote, "My
whole being, praise the Lord, and do not forget all His kindnesses."

But I focused only on the fact that I forget. All too often.

So, I ran.

I didn't actually jump on a boat out of town, but still I was
running. I got busier *doing* things for the Lord. I crammed my
calendar with serving at church and volunteering. I read a lot,
watched way too many reruns of *Law and Order,* and played oodles of
Solitaire on my smart phone.

But with all my busyness, I was not doing the assignment God
had given to me.

When I finally conquered that first battle and returned to
my writing desk, I let a different fear conquer me. After being so
wrapped up in striving to find the perfect words, I short-circuited my

writer's brain. I fell into self-doubt and went silent, again neglecting the call I felt on my life.

I was definitely running. Then I ran headlong into the book of Jonah.

As I read this short Old Testament book again, it seemed like the first time.

I have no recollection of when I first heard about Jonah. It was probably in a children's Sunday school class. I picture myself perched on a tiny wooden chair, using fat crayons to color a picture of the great fish while the teacher talked about the man who tried to run away from God's assignment.

Or maybe I first heard Jonah's name while snuggled in bed as Mother or my big sister read from the green children's Bible with a picture of Jesus and kids like me on the cover.

Either way, it was a long time ago.

Jonah's story had become so familiar it caused me to nod my head and say, "Oh, right. Jonah." as I'd hurried to move on from its few pages. I was tempted to think maybe other scriptures might have something new to tell me. Something designed to teach grown-ups rather than kids.

Something more modern.

If we hurry past Jonah, we miss a powerful book
with a lot of truth in its pages. We miss
a foreshadowing of a promise from God
so amazing it will take eternity to fully unfold.

But, if we hurry past Jonah, we miss a powerful book with a lot of truth in its pages. We miss a foreshadowing of a promise from God so amazing it will take eternity to fully unfold.

Maybe you've never heard of Jonah and don't have any idea of what I'm even talking about. Or it's possible you've only vaguely heard of the guy. If that's your situation, you're in for a treat.

I am convinced the Bible is the greatest treasure available to us because it is the divinely inspired Word of God. If this is a new concept for you, just come along on this Bible study journey. Ask God to reveal himself to you. If you find yourself wanting to scream "I'd rather die than obey," admit those feelings to God and ask him to show you why all of this matters so very much. And maybe you'll understand Jonah like I do because you'll see yourself on these pages of scripture.

In the coming chapters, we're going to dive deep into the book of Jonah. The individuals we will encounter act in surprising ways, turning our expectations on their heads. But as 2 Timothy 3:16 tells us, "All Scripture is inspired by God and is useful to teach us what is true and to make us realize what is wrong in our lives. It corrects us when we are wrong and teaches us to do what is right" (NLT)[1].

As we explore this ancient encounter, we will find huge lessons about God. Seeing Jonah angry and pouting will help us learn about the concepts of God's omnipresence, his unfailing love, his call to obedience, and our judgmental hearts. As we wade, then swim through the short book, we'll find it teaches a larger lesson about a God whose love is bigger and broader than the depths of our willful disobedience. The Bible Project's overview of Jonah said the book's ultimate purpose is to give us a mirror to look at our own lives.[2] Let's gaze intently into that mirror and ask God to show us what he sees in us at this moment and what he wants for our futures.

Once I realized I didn't want to wind up slimy and covered in seaweed in the belly of a huge fish, I committed words to paper and prayers for God to guide my brain, heart, and fingers in creating this work. I offer these pages to him for his honor and his glory. And I pray he will, through these chapters, reveal himself mightily and draw us all closer to him.

I am also praying for you, dear friend. As I write, I am asking God to teach us truths from his Word so we will leave these pages looking more like Jesus. The book of Jonah teaches us great truths about our struggle with obedience and helps us move past feeling guilty because of this struggle. Jonah's life offers us hope because his journey shows we don't have to be perfect or get everything right the first time for God to still use us.

I ask God to give us a revelation of his love and his plan for redemption and help us realize where our ancient Enemy has used hurt and unforgiveness as weapons against us. May we leave these pages with hearts open to God's plans for our lives and our world.

Let's grow in our trust of God, even when it hurts.

At the end of each chapter is a "Dive Deeper" section. These questions will be a great time for you to lean into God's presence and ask Him to reveal what the text is teaching you.

As you read, please remember I am a fellow journeyer —a woman who desperately wants to be faithful to God's calling and seek his face in Scripture. As we walk this path together, I invite you to nestle deep into the heavenly Father's loving arms. Ask God to open your eyes to truths he wants you to know. Let him clear a path for you. Allow him to bait the hook of your heart and guide you into the deep waters of his Word. This book —about a prophet who lived over 2,500 years ago —is as relevant today as when Jonah first told the tale of how God used a fish and a worm to change his heart.

Chapter 1

∽

When Obeying
Feels Overwhelming

(Scripture: Jonah 1-4)
(Don't worry, it's only about four pages.)

L et's be real:
living a life honoring to God can feel overwhelming.

As busy, modern women, we spend our days amid a whirlwind
of responsibility. My typical week includes juggling home, family,
career, and church. Throw in extras like community involvement
and serving others, friendships and self-care, and my heart is already
racing at the thought of handling it all.

Voices, responsibilities, emails, bills, items on the calendar, saving
for retirement, planning meals for the week, failing at planning meals
for the week, and mapping out steps to reach my dreams shout for

1

my attention. For me, and I'm guessing for you too, these things can build into a rising tide that threatens to swamp me. Sometimes I feel I don't do many of them well.

Maybe you can relate. Or you may have picked up this book because you've been hit between the eyes with the unexpected.

Divorce papers.

A devastating loss.

A disaster of some kind.

Your heart hurts, and you are so very tired.

Perhaps the waters of emotion threaten to overwhelm you, and you think you may break completely apart on the rocks in this battering sea.

Hope feels impossibly far away.

And when you turn to Scripture, you find it calls you to be holy, to rest, and to love others, even your enemies. Turning the other cheek may be the last thing you want to do. Even offering a small kindness can feel hard and leave us wondering how we're supposed to obey when it hurts so much.

Oh, precious friend, if you feel that way, you are in the right place. Draw close as we walk together into this book named Jonah.

Context is Key

In Jonah, we find a man who thought he knew best about justice and mercy and how he should get to decide who was deserving or not. Jonah was keeping score, and the people God put in his path simply didn't measure up in his eyes. He basically asked, *"God, what are you doing? Can't you see why I'm against this crazy plan?"*

Does that attitude sound familiar?

We'll dive deeper into those questions soon, but before we do, it will be helpful for us to get our bearings by exploring how the book of Jonah fits into Scripture as a whole. Think of it like a "You are Here" sign at your favorite outlet mall. In this case, it's important to know where Jonah is in context of the whole picture.

The first step of understanding our imagined map is to stand back and take the largest view possible. In Scripture, that means digging into its overarching purpose to understand why studying God's Word is important. And there's a great reason for us to do just that—through the divinely inspired words of the Bible, God has revealed himself to us. He wants us to know him.

If this is a new concept for you, come along on this journey. Walk with me through these chapters and allow God to speak to you.

The Bible is made up of 66 individual books written by 40 individuals; together, these books tell a grand story called the "metanarrative" about God and his plans for us. This overarching theme begins in Genesis with God creating the world and people. He set in place a plan for perfect fellowship between humankind (us) and himself. Then, sin entered the picture in Genesis 3. Sin is an act that goes against God's divine law.

Adam and Eve were rebellious. God had told them they could eat the fruit of any tree except one: the tree of the knowledge of good and evil. But that's exactly what the Serpent tempted them to do. Maybe they were like me and wanted to control their circumstances when God said to trust him. Maybe they thought some knowledge and experiences were being denied to them, that God was some kind of cosmic killjoy who didn't really have their best interests at heart. Our great-great-many-great ancestors didn't realize how much they'd already been given in the presence and fellowship they had with God. When the Serpent came asking, "Did God really say. . .?" they began to wonder, doubt, and try to reason things out for themselves rather than taking God at his word and trusting him. They didn't realize this serpent was actually Satan, who Jesus says is the Enemy who comes to kill, steal, and destroy the good God intends for us (John 10:10).

Sin separated humanity from God. Theologian R.C. Sproul's book The Holiness of God explains it well:

> Sin is cosmic treason. Sin is treason against a perfectly pure Sovereign. It is an act of supreme ingratitude toward the One to whom we owe everything, to the One who has given us life itself. Have you ever considered the deeper implications of the slightest sin, of the most minute peccadillo? What are we saying to our Creator when we disobey Him at the slightest point? We are saying no to the righteousness of God. We are saying, "God, Your law is not good. My judgment is better than Yours. Your authority does not apply to me. I am above and beyond Your jurisdiction. I have the right to do what I want to do, not what You command me to do."[3]

God is holy and pure, and our sin marred us, separating us from him. In fact, Romans 6:23 tells us, "The wages of sin is death." What Adam and Eve earned with their actions was death. It is what all of their offspring—including us—have earned as well. There was now a huge gulf between the Righteous Holy God and the people he created. In our natural state, we were helpless and hopeless.

The rest of the Bible, from the beginning of the Old Testament to the end of the New Testament, tells of the great plan God set in place to reveal the state we were in because of our sinful nature, then to draw us back to a restored relationship with him.

In the Old Testament, this restored relationship could only be maintained through an elaborate system of sacrifices that would temporarily cleanse God's people of sin and wrongdoing. God gave his chosen people laws or rules to follow about their behavior and how they were to approach God. Centuries later, the apostle Paul wrote, "No one can be made right with God by following the law. The law only shows us our sin." (Romans 3:20)

Jonah lived in these Old Testament times under the sacrificial system of the law. He was part of the group of people known as the Israelites. They were also known as God's chosen people. We will circle back to them. For now, let's return to the grand story of Scriptures, the metanarrative of what the Bible is all about.

Simply put, the Bible is about Jesus and the restoration he offers us through our belief in him. It's about his sovereignty, which is the supreme power and authority he holds as the Son of God, and how he is completely worthy of our praise, worship, and loving response to the hope he offers us when we trust in him.

You may be thinking, *Wait, Dawn! Wasn't the Old Testament written centuries before Jesus was born? How could it be about him? What makes you think that?*

Well, Jesus does.

In John 5:39, Jesus told the religious leaders of his day the Scriptures they studied so carefully "do, in fact, tell about me." At that moment in history, he was referring to what we now know as the Old Testament, but the same is true of the New Testament. All Scripture points to Jesus. As we study Jonah, we will look for what it tells us about Jesus and God's plan of redemption, although Jonah lived about eight centuries before Jesus was born on earth.

On our own and in a sinful state, humankind was without hope. But God had a solution to our problem, and that solution was Jesus. He came to earth as a baby born in Bethlehem. He was Emmanuel, meaning he was God who came down from heaven to live among us in human form. He became one of us to restore us to God. From our earth- and time-bound perspective, he lived on earth way after Jonah did, but Jesus is God the Son. He is eternal. The beginning words of the Gospel of John tell us:

> In the beginning there was the Word. The Word was with God, and the Word was God. He was with God in the beginning. All things were made by him, and nothing was made without him. In him there was life, and that life was the light of all people. The light shines in the darkness, and the darkness has not overpowered it. (John 1:1-5)

Jesus came to fulfill the Law (that system of sacrifices) and the teachings God had given through Scripture (Matthew 5:17). In the previous passage from John, he refers to Jesus as the Word of God. His sinless life, willing death, and triumphant resurrection became the ultimate fulfillment of the Law's sacrificial system. God, in the form of Jesus the Son, willingly gave his life to pay the price we could never pay on our own. His resurrection won the ultimate victory over sin and death. We are now offered complete restoration in a relationship with God through Jesus Christ.

Let's return to our "You are Here" map and focus on Jonah. This short book is one of 39 books that make up the Old Testament. Nearly half of those books are prophecy where God communicates with people through spokesmen called prophets. *The New Spirit-Filled Life Bible* defines prophet this way: A prophet is

> "One who proclaims or tells a message he has received; a spokesman, herald, announcer. A prophet is someone who announces a message at the direction of another (usually the Lord God)... The word can refer to false prophets and to prophets of false gods, but nearly always refers to Yahweh's commissioned spokesmen."[4]

The writings of the prophets are divided into two categories: The Major Prophets are Isaiah, Jeremiah, Lamentations, Ezekiel, and Daniel; and the Minor Prophets are Hosea, Joel, Amos, Obadiah, Jonah, Micah, Nahum, Habakkuk, Zephaniah, Haggai, Zechariah, and Malachi. This distinction between Major and Minor Prophets refers to the lengths of the books, not to the importance of their message.

As a prophet, Jonah was selected by God to speak for him and to carry his message to a specific group of people. Unlike most of the other Old Testament prophets, Jonah was not sent to the Israelites, but to a different group called the Ninevites.

Ancient Story, Timely Truths

We're going to move slowly through the pages of Jonah, but I encourage you to dive deep. Pause and think about what he experienced. Wonder with me what Jonah must have felt as the recorded events took place. We will also bring in other passages of Scripture to help us understand Jonah's faith journey, as well as our own.

Invite the Holy Spirit to guide and teach you what he wants to reveal about where you are at this moment. Jesus told his disciples, "But the helper, the Holy Spirit, whom the Father will send in my name, he will teach you all things and bring to your remembrance all that I have said to you" (John 14:26). Allow the Holy Spirit to teach you. Be on the lookout for the tiniest seeds of hope sprouting in your heart.

My prayer is for God to reveal how very well he understands us and our struggles, and how He wants to transform our hurts into part of his beautiful story of redemption. Come with me friend, bringing all your messy doubts and fears.

We will see how we can trust God, even with our angry, hurt, or unforgiving thoughts as we draw near to him. Lean into those questions. Ask God the things that keep you awake at night; then listen for his answer.

We will see how we can trust God, even with our angry, hurt, or unforgiving thoughts as we draw near to him. Lean into the hard questions. Ask God the questions that keep you awake at night; then listen for his answer. Hear and consider his words to Jonah and discover how they deepen our understanding of his plan to redeem not only the ancient Ninevites, but us and the Ninevites of our day.

By examining the life of this less-than-willing messenger, we will learn about God's unfailing love and discover how much he wants to use people like us, not in spite of our hurts, but often because of them. They have uniquely equipped us to share his love with others who are hurting, and even those who have hurt us.

Dive Deeper

Begin a conversation with God echoing Psalm 86:11:

Teach me your way, Lord,
that I may rely on your faithfulness;
give me an undivided heart,
that I may fear your name.

Spend a few moments reflecting on the following questions.
Write in the space below or journal about whatever God puts on your
heart. Ask God to give you wisdom and understanding.

Is the book of Jonah well-worn and familiar to you or are you
discovering it for the first time?

What do you think is main point of the book of Jonah? What do
you know about his story? What is your first impression about what
this book teaches?

What are your first impressions of Jonah based on what the
author shared in chapter 1?

One of the most famous parts of Jonah's story is the fact he ran away from God's command and was swallowed by a giant fish. Do you have your own "Jonah story"—a time when you ran from the Lord or from something you knew he wanted you to do? Jot down what that experience taught you or how you might be running from God now.

Prayer of Reflection

Heavenly Father, thank you for giving us the account of Jonah. As we read its truths, help us learn about you. We come with open hearts, knowing you have so much to teach us. Guide us as we seek truth in your Scripture. Give us wisdom, knowledge, and understanding. Help us not be afraid to look into the mirror that Jonah puts before us. Give us courage to respond as we sense you calling us. In Jesus' name we pray, amen.

Chapter 2

⤥

Just Who Is
This Guy Jonah?

(Scripture: Jonah 1:1-2)

I recently started a new job at the college where I worked two decades ago. I have been meeting a lot of people, learning names, and trying to get to know who the people are that make up my new work family. The process reminded me of a story I heard at a conference years ago. I'm sorry I can't recall the speaker's name, but I do remember the broad grin she wore as she talked in her slow southern drawl. I've paraphrased her story for you:

> "If you ask most people who a particular woman is, you'll get a neat, concise answer. Something like, 'That's Jane Smith. She's a banker.'"

The speaker stopped, planted her feet wide, and put her hands on her hips. Only then did she continue.

> "But ask a *southern* woman, and you're likely to get the *whole* story! There will probably be several generations of family connections mapped out before you're done. It'll sound something like, 'Oh, you know her—that's Jane Smith. Her mama is Sally Jones, Ed and Susie Parker's youngest. You remember, their homeplace was just outside of town by the old depot. Sally's sisters were the ones who married those Hawkins twins. Now, Jane and her husband, Bob—he's in insurance— well, can you believe they've been married for nearly twenty years now. What a beautiful wedding it was, too! They've got two kids. . .' And on and on the explanation might go."

That story made me laugh when I heard it, probably because it hit close to my rural Georgia home. But I've got to tell you, I find my southern self craving this level of detail when I read Scripture.

I want to get to know who a person really is. Did he have a wife and kids? Who were his parents? And their parents? When did they live? What jobs did they have?

These are actually good questions to give us a starting point for our study of Jonah. In this chapter, we will ask, just who was this guy? When did he live? And, as we southerners would put it, who were his people? Besides that, just who are these Ninevites?

Who is Jonah?

At first glance, we don't seem to have much information about Jonah, certainly not enough details to fill in a southern-style bio. We simply read, "The Lord spoke his word to Jonah, son of Amittai" (Jonah 1:1).

One way to better understand the meaning of Scripture is to explore the meaning of names. Think of the process you or your friends used when choosing names for your kids. Those names might honor parents or grandparents. Maybe you've chosen a maiden or other family name. Maybe it salutes a loved one, a friend, or comes from pop culture trends. Names can also reflect where you're from or what occupation one of your ancestors had.

Biblical names may also often reveal a person's character or the purpose they have been assigned by God. For example, in Genesis 5:17, God changed Abram's name, which meant "high father," to Abraham. The new name meant "father of a great multitude," and it became a reminder of a promise God had made to Abraham, one he now carried with him throughout each day.

So, what can we learn from Jonah's name?

According to *Smith's Bible Dictionary,* "Jonah" means "dove" and is sometimes referred to as "Jonas" in Greek.[5]

What do you think of when you hear the word "dove"? What images does the word bring to mind? Take a moment to write down your answer in the space below.

When I think of a dove, I picture beautiful white birds being released at weddings and their gray cousins hopping around our front yard on pretty spring days. I remember the words of Genesis 8 when Noah sent a dove out from the ark to see if there was dry land as the flood waters were receding.

But doves can make us think of more than just actual birds. Literarydevices.net describes one of the most common meanings: "The dove is a symbol of peace."[6] *Matthew Henry's Commentary on the Whole Bible* expands our understanding even more, saying, "Jonah signifies a dove, a proper name for all God's prophets, all His people, who ought to be harmless as doves, and to mourn as doves for the sins and calamities of the land."[7] Perhaps even more interesting is the idea that doves in Scripture are "seen multiple times to communicate God's long-reaching presence, security, and the promise of guaranteed hope."[8]

So, Jonah or "the dove" is understood to be a symbol of peace.

We are starting to understand that God seems to have carefully selected Jonah to go to the city of Nineveh. Let's add one more element to the mix. Verse 1 tellus us Jonah is the "son of Amittai." This Hebrew name means "my truth."[9]

In today's world, truth has gotten a raw deal. People encourage us to embrace our personal truth, but if what's true for you isn't also true for me, then how is it really true? Jonah's dad was named for something more permanent. A truth with a capital T that reflects the one true God and his Son, Jesus, who proclaimed himself to be the way, the truth, and the life (John 14:6). That's the truth, not a truth.

We can answer our first question, "Who is Jonah?" with the facts that he is a symbol of peace, a representation of God's presence, the bringer of promised hope, and the son of truth who was being sent to represent the God who is truth himself.

When Did Jonah Live?

The book that bears Jonah's name is not the only time he appears in Scripture. A passage in 2 Kings 14 gives us a few additional details about Jonah's work as a prophet. From verses 23-25, we learn he lived during the reign of Jeroboam II, who was king of Israel (or the Northern Kingdom) for forty-one years in the 8th century BC. He was king from 786 to 746 BC.

While Jonah lived during this time, the book that tells us about him was written much later.

> It is possible that some of the traditional materials taken over by the book were associated with Jonah at an early date, but the book in its present form reflects a much later composition. It was written after the Babylonian Exile (6th century BC), probably in the 5th or 4th century and certainly no later than the 3rd, since Jonah is listed among the Minor Prophets in the apocryphal book of Ecclesiasticus, composed about 190. Like the Book of Ruth, which was written at about the same period, it opposes the narrow Jewish nationalism characteristic of the period following the reforms of Ezra and Nehemiah with their emphasis on Jewish exclusivity. Thus the prophet Jonah, like the Jews of the day, abhors even the idea of salvation for the Gentiles. God chastises him for his attitude, and the book affirms that God's mercy extends even to the inhabitants of a hated foreign city.[10]

This means the book of Jonah was written somewhere between three and five centuries after the events it records.

We can also glean a few additional details about Jonah's life by carefully reading of his interaction with King Jeroboam II in 2 Kings 14: 24-25. This king, like many who ruled the Northern Kingdom, "did evil in the eyes of the Lord and did not turn away from any of the sins of Jeroboam son of Nebat, which he had caused Israel to commit" (2 Kings 14:24),

In verse 25, we learn Jonah is the one who delivered God's message to Jeroboam predicting the restoration of "the boundaries of Israel from Lebo Hamath to the Dead Sea." The verse adds this message was "spoken through his servant Jonah son of Amittai, the prophet from Gath-Hepher." (2 Kings 14:25) The town is also mentioned in Joshua 19:13 as one of the landmarks for the border of the inheritance given to the tribe of Zebulun. We will reflect on Jonah's hometown in a later chapter, but my southern heart likes the idea of him having a place to call home.

Who Were His People?

Jonah was part of a group known as the Israelites whose story makes up most of what we know as the Old Testament. The Israelites, also referred to as the Jews, were set apart as special to God because they were the descendants of a man named Abraham. We mentioned earlier in this chapter that God had given him a new name. As we read in Genesis 12, God called Abraham to leave his home and all he knew and to go where God would show him. So, Abraham went. He set out on a journey, obedient to God, and believed the promises God made to him—including that he would become the father of a great nation and so was given a new name. God established a covenant relationship with Abraham, and Abraham became different because of it.

A covenant is a special promise, and Scripture reveals God is a covenant-making God. *Holman Bible Dictionary* defines the word as follows:

> A pact, treaty, alliance, or agreement between two parties of equal or of unequal authority. The covenant or testament is a central, unifying theme in Scripture, God's covenants with individuals and the nation Israel finding final fulfillment in the new covenant in Christ Jesus. God's covenants can be understood by humans because they are modeled on human covenants or treaties.[11]

Part of the amazing beauty of God's covenant centers on this promise that involved unequal authority. We would have no right as humans to approach God on our own. Think of an impoverished beggar woman approaching a prince to propose marriage. Why would he ever agree to such a thing? Well, maybe you've seen enough Hallmark movies with a prince as a lead character to know the answer. Love. And that's exactly the case with God. He created us to love and to be in a relationship with him, and when the fellowship became broken, he took the initiative to restore it.

He was the only one who could.

Another remarkable fact about this covenant is the terms of the agreement. In Abraham's day, making a covenant was serious business; the parties were agreeing to terms and adding "may I be punished severely if I break this promise." But God did something unheard of in his covenant with Abraham: he added that he would take the punishment if Abraham and his descendants were the ones to break the covenant relationship.

Don't miss that God is all-knowing, so of course He knew Abraham's descendants would break the covenant. He entered into the agreement anyway and had the perfect plan for restoration. John 3:16 tells us, "God loved the world so much that he gave his one and only Son so that whoever believes in him may not be lost, but have eternal life." The seed of this promise of eternal life took root in the covenant between God and Abraham. God's covenant set Abraham's natural descendants—the Jewish people—apart as special and made them distinct from other non-Jewish peoples of the world (often referred to in Scripture as Gentiles). Because of the covenant relationship, the Jews were to act differently, and the law was given later to provide specific instructions on how to maintain that relationship. They rebelled time and time again, and as a consequence of their disobedience were often defeated by enemies God allowed to rise to power.

This is where Jonah fits into the story. Jonah was told by God to go and preach to one of Israel's great enemies: the empire of Assyria. Most specifically, the capital city of Nineveh. This is one of the earliest examples of God sending a message specifically to people who were not of Jewish descent.

The book of Jonah is unique. The books that teach us about other prophets focus mainly on the word of God given through His messengers, but Jonah focuses on this prophet's experiences and attitudes rather than on what God had to say to the Ninevites.

Jonah's job was to take God's message to the people of Nineveh, and Jonah understood God would be offering them a chance to repent. There was just one problem: Jonah didn't want to see Israel's enemies receive forgiveness. He didn't want any part of this plan.

Who Were the Ninevites?

While we may find ourselves wondering who the Ninevites were, this is not a question Jonah would have needed answered. He knew exactly who they were, and he didn't like them one bit. To help us understand why Jonah was reluctant, the following is a quick summary of what we know about the Ninevites.

Nineveh was an ancient city built by Nimrod, a descendant of Noah's grandson Cush as we're told in Genesis 10:11, and the city had become "the capital of the ancient kingdom and empire of Assyria."[12] Nineveh was located in what today is northern Iraq. Many online articles described the Assyrian empire as filled with cruelty. One article depicts Nineveh as "Sin City."[13] The Ninevites were enemies of Israel and were not part of God's covenant people. These outsiders were hostile to the Israelites and their worship of God. They were known for being ruthless to their enemies.

In addition, I imagine they chased after their own interests and craved pleasure and national prominence and had little firsthand knowledge of the one true God, who was foreign to them at best. Their sins, as this second verse of Jonah shows us, had reached all the way to heaven.

There's no doubt Jonah knew the job God was giving him. The assignment was clear. And Jonah knew the call came from God. *Matthew Henry's Commentary on the Whole Bible* suggests, "He has been before acquainted with the word of the Lord and knew his voice from that of a stranger."[14]

God called Jonah to take his message of judgment to the Ninevites. But Jonah knew this judgment came with the possibility of forgiveness. He'd been taught the words of Psalm 32 where David talked about God's willingness to forgive sins. We will soon see that

Jonah fled from God's call and landed in what might rank as the most unexpected place of all: the inside of a great fish.

Jonah's struggle tells us much more than just another fish tale. This book gives us a clear picture of God's plan of redemption and asks us to examine ourselves to see if we will trust him enough to join him in it.

Are We like Jonah?

As I am growing older, the Holy Spirit is revealing more and more truth about Jonah. Little girl Dawn only understood him to be a man who disobeyed God. But now I understand obeying doesn't simply feel hard, it can be extremely difficult.

The news of recent days has been filled with fresh conflict for the modern-day nation of Israel. As I watch the violence and anger unfold on my television inside my safe, warm home, I feel fresh sympathy for Jonah's reluctance. God told him to take a message of forgiveness to people who were enemies of Jonah's homeland. They were brutal, had killed people like him, and would likely do the same or worse to a prophet who showed up telling them they needed to repent. What God asked of Jonah was a hard thing.

Obedience is a gift we give to God because he is worthy of our trust, faith, and actions to accomplish what he has asked of us. We choose to obey because it honors him.

We aren't asked to obey because it is easy or because we understand God's plan. Obedience is a gift we give to God because he is worthy of our trust, faith, and actions to accomplish what he has asked of us. We choose to obey because it honors him.

Jonah was asked to go to the enemies of his people. Who is the person who comes to your mind when you hear the word *enemy*? The hardest one for you to picture forgiving? To wish God's absolute best for? Those questions might cause some uncomfortable soul-squirming. Our minds possibly flashed up faces connected to scars we carry.

Those mental pictures may be different for each of us:

- A boss who tried to block career advancement
- Friends who disappeared from our lives without explanation or maybe with heartbreaking scenes
- A husband who promised to love and cherish, then didn't
- A business partner who stole from a shared venture
- A colleague, believed to be a friend, who turned out to be a backstabber
- Someone who tried to injure you physically
- Someone who did injure you, physically and emotionally
- The drunk driver who killed a loved one
- The person who murdered a loved one in cold blood
- People who mistreated you because of your gender, skin color, nationality, or religion
- National enemies, like the Ninevites were to Jonah, who long to see you and everyone you love destroyed

While our lists will vary based on our experiences, we all have been touched by hurts. Memories of those painful moments are still capable of causing a gnawing ache deep within us if we leave them unexamined and unforgiven.

Had Jonah suffered personal loss at the hands of the Ninevites? While there's no indication of that in Scripture, he almost certainly had seen and heard about how they treated other Israelites. As we look into Jonah's story, we must be willing to see our own hard times and the reflection of people we may want to dislike. Those reflected faces may make us want to cry out to the heavens, "Surely, God, your offer of forgiveness doesn't include _____?"

For Jonah, perhaps no group would have more perfectly filled in this blank than the Ninevites. These people were known for brutal treatment of captives. They excelled at things like oppression and destruction. They were outside the covenant promise God had made with Abraham and, according to Jewish law, not beneficiaries of the blessings of God.

Earlier in his work as a prophet, Jonah had prophesied God would grant King Jeroboam II restoration of land lost because of the previous king's rebellion, and 2 Kings 14:24 tells us this prophecy came to be. Now, in Jonah 1:2, God has a new assignment for his prophet: "Get up, go to the great city of Nineveh and preach against it, because I see the evil things they do."

In Jonah 1:2 God is sending his prophet to preach against the city, but I believe he wants Jonah to preach to the people of Nineveh. Like Jonah, we might find ourselves confused and asking hard questions like, *Why would God send a prophet to people who were not part of his covenant relationship with Israel? After all, these Ninevites were enemies of his chosen people.*

Well, when we look at Jonah's situation from this early point in his journey, we don't know yet. But we should always read Scripture as part of the larger narrative of God's plan to restore fellowship with humanity. In our study of Scripture and even in our own lives, we don't always understand God's motives. We can ask him, but he is under no obligation to tell us the reason. Theologian J.I. Packer put it this way:

For the truth is that God in His wisdom, to make and keep us humble and to teach us to walk by faith, has hidden from us almost everything that we should like to know about the providential purposes which He is working out in the churches and in our own lives.[15]

Packer referenced Ecclesiastes 11:5, "You don't know where the wind will blow, and you don't know how a baby grows inside the mother. In the same way, you don't know what God is doing or how he created everything."

What are we to do when we don't understand what God is up to? It's simple really.

We are to trust him.

As we go forward in Jonah's story, ask whether the prophet trusted God or relied on his own reasoning. What about us?

Dive Deeper

What does the idea of God establishing a covenant with his people mean to you personally? Why do you think God would enter into this covenant with the Israelites when he knew they would break it?

Why do you think Jonah might not have wanted to see the Ninevites forgiven by God?

Did someone come to mind as you read about Jonah's struggle to want the best for people he considered to be enemies?

Do you find it hard to trust God when you don't understand why he is asking you to do something? Journal about your feelings and write a prayer asking God to help you grow in this area.

Prayer of Reflection

Sovereign Lord, we confess we don't always understand your purposes or why you've asked us to do something difficult like sharing your love with those who have or almost certainly would hurt us. Lord, give us eyes to see your heart in these moments. Help us to lean into you, trusting your goodness and your care for us. In Jesus' name we pray, amen.

Chapter 3

"I'd Rather Die than Obey"

(Scripture: Jonah 1:2-3)

After travel reopened following the Covid-19 pandemic, a friend
shared on social media about feeling called to talk with a woman
sitting next to her in public. As soon as she felt the tugging on her
heart, she began to think, *I'm not going to talk with her; she might think
I'm strange.* Soon, all kinds of reasons were racing through her mind,
trying to convince her obeying was not the right thing to do.

Maybe the lady wanted to be left alone.

Maybe she is afraid of strangers or the possibility of getting Covid-19.

She could feel threatened or think my friend was weird.

Thankfully, my friend pushed through the noise to pray. She
asked God what she should do and again felt the urge to strike up a
conversation.

Turns out, the woman in question was hurting deeply. She was juggling the loss of a loved one, physical separation from her family, and learning to navigate life on her own. Because of my friend's obedience, the lady left the encounter having felt seen by God. Their brief moments together let light shine into the darkness of the woman's current circumstances.

My friend could have said no. She could have chosen her comfort zone over being a healing balm to this woman's spirit. She could have missed the blessing of being used in God's plan of grace and love.

What Would Jonah Choose?

In Chapter 2, we learned some facts about Jonah and saw the job God gave him. Let's look again at the call Jonah received:

> "Get up, go to the great city of Nineveh, and preach against it, because I see the evil things they do." (Jonah 1:2)

The question remains: "Will Jonah obey?"

In our Christian walk, it can sometimes be hard to discern exactly what God is telling us, to determine which path is the one meant for us to take. Jonah did not have this problem. The Bible makes it plain Jonah knew exactly what God was telling him to do. But Jonah didn't want to do it. He chose disobedience.

Complete and total, drastic disobedience.

Through his actions, Jonah basically told God, *I'd rather die than do what you've asked.*

I'd rather die than obey you.

It's right there in Jonah 1:3:

> "But Jonah got up to run away from the Lord by going to Tarshish. He went to the city of Joppa, where he found a ship that was going to the city of Tarshish. Jonah paid for the trip and went aboard, planning to go to Tarshish to run away from the Lord."

Note the repeated words: "to run away from the Lord." Jonah didn't want to be part of God's plan for redeeming Nineveh. He wanted to escape.

God told Jonah to go.

Jonah simply said no.

God's plan didn't seem right to Jonah, and he wanted absolutely no part in it. Justice—or at least what passed for justice in Jonah's mind—may have been a factor in his actions. Jonah had heard how evil the Ninevites were. Maybe he had friends and family whose loved ones had suffered under the Ninevites' brutality. Jonah may have thought about the people God was sending him to and said, *"Nope. I'm not going to be part of offering them forgiveness."* Jonah weighed the Ninevites on his personal scale of justice and decided they didn't deserve God's grace and mercy. We'll see more about this later in the book of Jonah, but for now, let's focus on what he did instead of obeying.

Jonah Disobeyed Drastically!

Scholars tell us it's possible Jonah was in his hometown of Gath-hepher when he got the Lord's command. Gath-hepher is near Nazareth in Israel. God was sending him to Nineveh, "located east of the Tigris in modern-day Iraq, more than five hundred miles east of Jonah's hometown.[16]

Jonah got up alright, and he went. But he headed west, via the port city of Joppa. There, he hopped a charter and set sail for Tarshish over 2,500 miles from Israel in the opposite direction from where God had sent him.

Listen to how *Smith's Bible Commentary* explains the significance of Jonah's route:

> Ninevah was east and north from Israel. Jonah went down and caught a ship going west. He is going to run from the call of God. Now God is calling him to go and preach to the Gentiles, something he did not want to do. Felt this nationalist spirit—salvation is of the Jews; it is not for the Gentiles. He did not want to go to the Gentiles. And so he went to Joppa to escape the call of God to go to the Gentiles.
>
> It is interesting that several years later in this very same port city of Joppa, as Peter was on the rooftop of the house of Simon the tanner, that he first saw this sheet in a vision let down from heaven; tied at the corners with all manner of beast and creeping things on it. And the Lord said to Peter, "Rise, Peter, kill and eat." And when Peter objected saying, "Lord, I've never eaten anything that was unclean or common." God said, "Don't call that common which I have cleansed." After this thing happened three times, Peter wondered, "What in the world does this mean?" And the Lord spoke to him

and said, "There are some men now down at
the gate inquiring for you. Go with them and
don't ask any questions. I'll tell you what to say."
And there in Joppa is where Peter was called to
take the gospel to the Gentiles. Interesting how
things always seem to come back.

It was to Joppa that Jonah ran to catch a ship to
escape preaching to the Gentiles. It was at Joppa
that the Lord called Peter and said to go to the
Gentiles. And the door of the gospel was open
to the Gentiles as God dealt with Peter there in
Joppa.[17]

Joppa, which today is known as Jaffa and is a suburb of Tel
Aviv, was thirty-five miles from Jerusalem and served as its primary
connection to the sea. This city was Jonah's first stop on his flight
away from God's call. A few hundred years later, the apostle Peter
was in this city when he had a very significant dream. Perhaps Joppa
appears in both Jonah's and Peter's experiences because it was a
major hub of travel, much like Atlanta's Hartsfield-Jackson Airport,
which is about an hour away from my home. The ATL (as the
airport is known) is often the first stop for people from this region
to get anywhere they want to go. For Jonah, where he wanted to go
was away from where God sent him, and Joppa was his launching
point. From there he ran away from God's plan to share his love
with people who were outside those descended from Abraham. But
the city of Joppa hints at God's redemptive power at work. Almost
1,000 years later, this city would become the place where Peter was
convinced in a dream to share the gospel with non-Jews (Acts 10).

That makes Joppa an important part of my story too. I am one of those non-Jewish people who would be able to receive the good news about Jesus because of Peter's obedience.

Jonah set sail from Joppa on the eastern side of the Mediterranean Sea and headed west toward Tarshish, which is believed by some scholars to have been the southern tip of what is now Spain or could have even been modern-day England. Let those facts sink in for a moment. This is in the 8th century BC. The city of Tarshish had to be on or near the far reaches of what was the known world at the time.

> Jonah was arising and seeking to flee from the presence of the Lord, heading for Tarshish. Biblical scholars are divided as to the location of Tarshish. Some say it is a part of Spain; others say it is England. The preponderance of scholars seem to favor England. Wherever Tarshish was, it was the furthest outpost of the known world at that time. It was the jumping off point. You can't go any farther than Tarshish from the civilized world. It was the end. It was as far as you could go. Beyond Tarshish lay that wild, boisterous Atlantic, and out there somewhere that precipice, that chasm, that point where the ships just dropped off into oblivion. No ships ever came back from their voyages on the Atlantic. They surely must have gone over the edge of the world someplace and disappeared. So Tarshish was as far as you dared to go, and that is where Jonah was heading. "I'm going to get as far away from

God as I can. I'll head for Tarshish. I'll hide from
the call of God, from the presence of the Lord."

Now, it was a deceptive lie for Jonah to think
that he could escape God. It was a deceptive
lie to think that he would be better off running
from God and running from the call of God.
That was a deception and that was a lie. Many
people live under that same delusion. "I would
be better off if I could just escape the will of
God for my life. I can determine what is best
for me better than God can determine. I know
what is better for the people of God than God
does. If I go to Nineveh and preach the gospel to
those Gentiles, if they believe and repent, then
God being the softy that He is, being merciful as
He is, will probably forgive them and not destroy
them. And if they are not destroyed then they
are apt to destroy our people. I'm not going. I'm
heading for Tarshish. I'm going to get as far away
from Nineveh as is humanly possible."

So he went down to Joppa to flee to Tarshish
from the presence of the Lord. And he got a ship
and paid the fare; went down in the hull to flee
from the presence of the Lord.[18]

Jonah was trying to go as far as humanly possible in the opposite
direction from Nineveh, hoping to evade God's plan.

What Did Fleeing Feel Like?

In my mind's eye, the Mediterranean Sea is intensely beautiful as the boat carrying Jonah sets sail on his journey to escape God. Picture him there, a breeze tousling his hair. I wonder how he must have felt as the boat edged further away from the shore.

Was he thinking about the job God had told him to do and how he wasn't about to have anything to do with it?

Was he pleased with himself, thinking he'd done a good job of dodging his assignment as the ship set out under gorgeous skies, across the deep blue waters of the Mediterranean?

Or did he feel guilty knowing he was being disobedient?

Was he raging in his heart about the audacity of God asking him to preach to those people? Did he remind God in prayer (or at least rehearse arguments in his head) about all the things the Ninevites had done wrong, pointing out all the reasons why fire and brimstone raining on them was exactly what they deserved?

It's not too hard to imagine him possibly huffing around as he stowed his gear in the spot he was given. Did he unpack his extra shirt while unloading his anger and resentment?

Or was fear driving Jonah to flee? Did he think the Ninevites would have him drawn and quartered or whatever horrible punishment they'd invent to deal with troublemakers? Maybe Jonah pictured himself preaching God's Word, then being called to account for what he'd said. Maybe he could envision government officials swooping down in their time's equivalent of black-clad, tinted-windowed chariots to take him away, knowing he'd never be seen again.

Nope. Not me, he might have thought. *I'm not ending up somewhere dark and scary, all alone with no hope of escaping with my life.*

Where was his faith? Did he trust in his own reasoning as a ship and a crew carried him to parts unknown? Did he trust in his ideas and knowledge about the Ninevites? Was he convinced he was right and God was wrong?

What does it mean to obey?

Jonah had a choice. My friend had a choice. You and I have a choice. When God invites us into his family, will we respond or decide all this spiritual stuff doesn't really apply to us? When God gives an assignment to those of us who believe in him, will we obey? Will we come away on a sunny Saturday in February to write words that can help us draw closer to God? Will we have the conversation with a stranger? Will we carry the message of God's love and forgiveness anywhere he might send us? Will we trust him even when it hurts?

Jonah had a choice. My friend had a choice. You and I have a choice. When God invites us into his family will we respond or decide all this spiritual stuff doesn't really apply to us? When God gives an assignment to those of us who believe in him, will we obey?. . . Will we trust him even when it hurts?

Obedience is a concept most of us generally understand. We likely learned it from an early age as the grownups in our lives set rules and limits for us. We either obeyed or faced the consequences of disobedience. Our responses may have changed as we entered our teenage years and started exerting our independence, but we would still find ourselves with a choice: do what was asked of us or don't—and face the consequences.

As adults, we know there are rules that must be obeyed. A simple example is the speed limit posted on your daily drive. While someone with a heavy foot may fudge on the upper limit, if the infraction is excessive, it could be met with consequences. That could be a speeding ticket, a fine, or if the offense is bad enough, loss of driving privileges.

The question of our obedience isn't limited to our time behind the wheel. At work, our employers likely have handbooks or spoken guidelines to tell us the rules of the relationship. These cover a wide range of situations including how vacation time is to be handled, what hours we're expected to work, and how we are to represent the organization through our actions and interactions. Failure to adequately obey the rules can lead to a reprimand, a plan of corrective action, or even termination from our position.

In these situations and thousands more, we have a choice: will we obey what is asked of us or not? We may find ourselves obeying because we feel we must and not because we want to. In that case, obedience can easily become transactional and more focused on our self-interests than on mutual respect. That attitude might be okay in the case of a speed limit posted by a local government, but what about obedience to God?

Is our obedience just a question of doing something he asks of us to avoid bad consequences? Heavens no! Parents wouldn't want their children to obey simply out of fear or some twisted idea of reciprocity. The idea isn't to teach your daughter that if she does what you want and follows all the rules, then she'll get gifts—or worse, that then you'll love her.

That's not what God wants for his daughters either.

I love this passage from a sermon by the 19th century English minister Charles Spurgeon. It helps us see that, for a Christ-follower, obedience grows out of the relationship we have with God as our Father and Christ as our elder brother:

> Obedience is the grand object of the work of grace in the hearts of those who are chosen and called: they are to become obedient children, conformed to the image of the Elder Brother, with whom the Father is well pleased.
>
> The obedience that comes of faith is of a noble sort. The obedience of a slave ranks very little higher than the obedience of a well-trained horse or dog, for it is tuned to the crack of the whip. Obedience which is not cheerfully rendered is not the obedience of the heart, and consequently is of little worth before God. If the man obeys because he has no opportunity of doing otherwise, and if, were he free, he would at once become a rebel—there is nothing in his obedience. The obedience of faith springs from a principle within and not from compulsion without. It is sustained by the mind's soberest reasoning and the heart's warmest passion. The man reasons with himself that he ought to obey his Redeemer, his Father, his God; and, at the same time, the love of Christ constrains him so to do, and thus what argument suggests

affection performs. A sense of great obligation, an apprehension of the fitness of obedience, and spiritual renewal of heart, work an obedience which becomes essential to the sanctified soul. Hence, it is not relaxed in the time of temptation, nor destroyed in the hour of losses and sufferings. Life has no trial which can turn the gracious soul from its passion for obedience; and death itself doth but enable it to render an obedience which shall be as blissful as it will be complete. Yes, this is a chief ingredient of heaven—that we shall see the face of our Lord and serve him day and night in his temple. Meanwhile, the more fully we obey at this present, the nearer we shall be to his temple-gate. May the Holy Spirit work in us, so that, by faith— like Abraham— we may obey!

I preach to you, at this time, obedience— absolute obedience to the Lord God; but I preach the obedience of a child, not the obedience of a slave; the obedience of love, not of terror; the obedience of faith, not of dread.[19]

God wants us to obey because we love him and want to please him, not because we are fearful of lightning bolts flying from the sky. As Spurgeon so beautifully and clearly put it, "Obedience which is not cheerfully rendered is not the obedience of the heart, and consequently is of little worth before God."

I want my obedience to matter to God, and I imagine you do as well. But what does it look like for us to obey?

Defining True Obedience

When God calls us to an assignment, we always have a choice. Will we obey immediately? Will we delay? Or will we be like Jonah and completely disobey? Only one of those choices represents true obedience, and that is moving forward with what God has asked when he asks. Let's return to Genesis and the life of Abraham for an example of what this looks like in practice.

In Genesis 12:1, we read that the Lord told Abram (before his name was changed) to "leave your country, your relatives, and your father's family, and go to the land I will show you." Then verse 4 says simply,

> "So Abram left Haran as the Lord had told him."

God said it, so Abraham did it. That's obedience.

Abraham had a second test of his obedience when he was asked to offer his son Isaac as a sacrifice. This was the son he'd been promised, had longed for, prayed for, and even tried to trick his way toward. Now, he was being asked to give up this beloved son. And I know this is a confusing example because why would God want Abraham to sacrifice his son? I don't believe he did. I believe God was testing Abraham's faith, to see if he would give up the most precious thing in his life if the Lord asked him to. Let's look at the passage in Genesis.

> After these things God tested Abraham's faith.
> God said to him, "Abraham!"
>
> And he answered, "Here I am."

Then God said, "Take your only son, Isaac, the son you love, and go to the land of Moriah. Kill him there and offer him as a whole burnt offering on one of the mountains I will tell you about."

Abraham got up early in the morning and saddled his donkey. He took Isaac and two servants with him. After he cut the wood for the sacrifice, they went to the place God had told them to go. On the third day Abraham looked up and saw the place in the distance. He said to his servants, "Stay here with the donkey. My son and I will go over there and worship, and then we will come back to you."

Abraham took the wood for the sacrifice and gave it to his son to carry, but he himself took the knife and the fire. So he and his son went on together.

Isaac said to his father Abraham, "Father!"

Abraham answered, "Yes, my son."

Isaac said, "We have the fire and the wood, but where is the lamb we will burn as a sacrifice?"

Abraham answered, "God will give us the lamb for the sacrifice, my son."

So Abraham and his son went on together and came to the place God had told him about. Abraham built an altar there. He laid the wood on it and then tied up his son Isaac and laid him on the wood on the altar. Then Abraham took his knife and was about to kill his son.

But the angel of the Lord called to him from heaven and said, "Abraham! Abraham!"

Abraham answered, "Yes."

The angel said, "Don't kill your son or hurt him in any way. Now I can see that you trust God and that you have not kept your son, your only son, from me."

Then Abraham looked up and saw a male sheep caught in a bush by its horns. So Abraham went and took the sheep and killed it. He offered it as a whole burnt offering to God, and his son was saved. So Abraham named that place The Lord Provides. Even today people say, "On the mountain of the Lord it will be provided."

The angel of the Lord called to Abraham from heaven a second time and said, "The Lord says, 'Because you did not keep back your son, your only son, from me, I make you this promise by

my own name: I will surely bless you and give
you many descendants. They will be as many as
the stars in the sky and the sand on the seashore,
and they will capture the cities of their enemies.
Through your descendants all the nations on the
earth will be blessed, because you obeyed me.'"
(Genesis 22:1-19)

Did you see Abraham's faith in action throughout that passage?
He was told to do something extremely difficult, yet, in verse 3, he
got up "early the next morning" and started on the journey. God had
told him to sacrifice his son, but Abraham trusted God. He told his
servants in verse 5, "We will worship and then we will come back to
you." When Isaac asked about the lamb for the sacrifice, Abraham
replied in verse 8, "God himself will provide the lamb for the burnt
offering, my son." Abraham knew the heart of God and trusted him,
even when God didn't reveal the entire plan or the circumstances
were completely beyond understanding.

In Romans 4:3, we read:

> What does Scripture say? "Abraham believed
> God, and it was credited to him as righteousness."

Hebrews 11:17-19 adds to our understanding:

> It was by faith that Abraham, when God tested
> him, offered his son Isaac as a sacrifice. God
> made the promises to Abraham, but Abraham
> was ready to offer his own son as a sacrifice.
> God had said, "The descendants I promised
> you will be from Isaac." Abraham believed that

God could raise the dead, and really, it was as if
Abraham got Isaac back from death.

He believed God because he knew God's heart. God had been
faithful and true, and Abraham knew he could be trusted when what
he asked didn't make sense. Abraham was willing to offer his son
because he had confidence God would work things out, even if it
meant they needed a miracle. That's the kind of obedience, the kind
of trust, and the kind of faith I want to grow in my life.

You might think it was easier for Abraham to obey. He was just
being asked to move—admittedly away from everything he knew—
but it wasn't like he was being asked to deal with evil people. Well,
let's look to 20th century history for another example from the
life of a young Dutch lady, the daughter of a watchmaker. Corrie
Ten Boom[20] and her family saw how the Jewish people were being
mistreated in their hometown in the years leading up to what would
become World War II. Rather than turning a blind eye or praying
for God to send someone else to help, the Ten Booms opened their
home to Jewish refugees. They hid as many in their home as they
could, saving families and children from the Nazis. Eventually, the
Ten Booms were found out, and their entire family was arrested.
Corrie and her sister were sent to Ravensbruck, a concentration
camp for women in northern Germany. There, her sister died, and
Corrie, along with the other women who survived, was horribly
mistreated. One particular guard stood out in her mind as having
been exceptionally cruel in a place that was the definition of extreme
cruelty.

Years later, after Corrie had survived the camp and began
sharing her story of how God had drawn her to himself and cared
for her even in the darkest of days, Corrie encountered that guard

again. He had become a Christian and wanted Corrie's forgiveness. Can you imagine the ocean of feelings that must have engulfed her in that moment? Can you feel the bitterness and hate that surely nipped at her heels, whispering for her to repay evil with evil? Would she be obedient to God's call for forgiveness? Take a moment and sit with the difficulty of the situation she found herself in. A man who'd been incredibly cruel to her, her sister, and so many other women now asked Corrie for forgiveness and mercy that he had not shown. What would she do?

Well, if she was like Jonah, she would have run away as fast as she could. That's not how Corrie's story ended. She knew that Jesus, who had been such a strong hiding place of protection for her spiritually during her time in Ravensbruck, had also suffered terribly at the hands of men. But his prayer from the cross had been, "Father, forgive them, because they do not know what they are doing" (Luke 23:34). Corrie knew she needed to offer that same type of forgiveness. In the Lord's Prayer, Jesus taught us to pray for God to forgive us in the same way we forgive others. He expects us to forgive in difficult moments because we are following in Jesus' footsteps. That's what Corrie Ten Boom's obedience teaches us.

Delayed Obedience or Disobedience with a Nice Coat of Lipstick?

We've looked at Jonah's complete disobedience and Abraham's immediate obedience. We've fast-forwarded a couple of millennia and seen Corrie's faithful forgiveness. We may find ourselves wondering, isn't there something in the middle we can choose—a choice that's not so difficult to make? What about delayed obedience? Would that work?

There was an urgency to the call Jonah received. God wanted him in today's language to get up and get a move on. Let's dig in a little about this. What do we do when we "get up"? Most days, I like to have my first cup of coffee before tackling anything too strenuous! Taking my time helps me adjust to the new day, easing into the coming harder assignments. I don't think God minds my morning coffee, but this slow start isn't the kind of reaction we should have when we feel God giving us an assignment. We should be quick to obey.

God may give us second chances, and third, and fourth chances. I started working on this book years ago but needed to walk through some difficult times to understand more fully the lessons I am sharing with you. I believe God used the delay to prepare me, drawing me closer to him and helping me overcome fear and live in faith. But we must be careful not to expect God to always give us another chance. He is sovereign. He decides whether he will or will not continue to use us.

Delaying may seem like obeying, but we need to examine our hearts to know if we are truly obeying or if we are just stalling. Was I hiding behind fear instead of trusting God? I've prayed and asked God to help me know and to forgive the parts that were delay or disobedience.

Imagine God tells a woman to go as a missionary to another country. She might want to talk with others to confirm the calling. She might spend time gathering facts and doing research on the area she would be going to and the people she'd be serving. She'd probably like to know where to stay and would want to make reservations and raise money. She would definitely want time to read a book or two or some online articles to help her know what to expect. While there's nothing wrong with preparing to fulfill the call we've received—and a lot of those choices I described may be steps toward faithful obedience—we must examine our motives.

We can ask ourselves questions like:

- Are our actions moving us along the path of obedience or have we moved into over-planning and over-strategizing?
- Is this knowledge-seeking where we are placing our hope and trust rather than in God?
- Are we counting on God or all of our research and preparation to take care of us?
- Are these actions allowing us to put off obeying in the hope God will let us off the hook?

The problem with "delayed obedience" is it can often be disobedience with a nice coat of lipstick. The issue, of course, is our hearts. We must honestly answer the question: are we seeking to obey God, or are we allowing ourselves to be bossed around by fear or that voice in our heads telling us God can't really use someone like us? We need to prayerfully bring our motives to God and ask him to help us move forward in true obedience.

Disobedience: Passive or Drastic

I've spent a lot of time thinking about Jonah on that ship as Joppa faded away into the horizon. I wonder how he passed the time. Was he trying to avoid thinking about God's call? Did he try to keep all things Nineveh-related as far away from conscious thought as possible? Was he able to pray, or did his prayers feel swallowed up by the sea air? Did he offer to help the crew so he would be tired at night and might be able to sleep a little?

What did running from God look like for Jonah? What did it feel like?

Of course, we'll never know the answer to those questions, at least not until we get to heaven, and I'm not sure it will matter so much then. I mean, if I headed out of town and hopped on a boat to the end of the world, I'm pretty sure my husband, my boss, and my mortgage lender would have questions! But considering what Jonah was thinking and feeling is important.

Because I've been angry.

I've looked at people and thought I was better than they were.

I've been afraid.

I've tried to hide.

And I've even tried a few times to tell God how much better my plans were than his. Oh, maybe those weren't my exact words, but the same spirit was there when I complained about his timing or my calling. I can't help but reflect on those years I spent doing things I knew in my heart weren't the best things God had planned for me. The core of my calling was writing, and I wanted to get as far away from this chair and computer screen as possible. Because I thought if I were busy enough (like maybe Jonah tried to be on the ship) then God might say, "Oh, it's okay, Dawn. You do all those things and somebody else can do this writing thing."

That is not how things worked out for me, and it's not how they worked out for Jonah.

Jonah's disobedience was dramatic. He left no doubt and no room to change his mind. He was willing to leave everything and sail away.

Our disobedience can be dramatic too. We can rage at the heavens and run away from God's calling. But we can also have a less drastic response that winds up with exactly the same results: saying no to God.

Jonah's disobedience was dramatic. He left no doubt and no room to change his mind. He was willing to leave everything and sail away. Our disobedience can be dramatic too. We can rage at the heavens and run away from God's calling. But we can also have a less drastic response that winds up with exactly the same results: saying no to God.

What are the assignments we may be answering with a drastic or a passive no?

I'm not going to lead the small group; I don't know enough to be in charge. Someone might ask hard questions.

I'm not going to offer forgiveness to that family member who hurt my feelings. I have a right to be angry.

I'm not going to obey you God; I don't know why you want to control me anyway?

I'm not going to be part of carrying your message of forgiveness to _____. Don't you remember what they've done? I am staying right here, holding on to my anger and resentment.

Jonah is the epitome of drastic disobedience. He went in the complete opposite direction from where he was sent. He determined to run away from God. In the next chapter, we will see how well that worked out for him.

Dive Deeper

What difference do you see in Abraham's reaction to God's instruction in Genesis 22 and Jonah's in Jonah 1:1-3?

Take a moment to prayerfully consider if there has been a time (or lots of times) when God asked you to do something you didn't want to do. Maybe it looked like God telling you to stand up when you saw injustice, but instead you listened to the gnawing thoughts saying you didn't need to be the one to do anything. Maybe, like in my friend's case, God called you to talk with or help a stranger, but you didn't want to be thought of as weird or nosy. Maybe God wanted you to use your talents for his glory, but instead you were like me and listened to fear saying you weren't good enough.

What was your response? Immediate obedience, delayed obedience, or disobedience? Why did you make that choice? Write down what God is telling you about your choice.

What do you think God wants you to know about times when you've been disobedient?

What do you think of the idea that delayed obedience can often be disobedience with a nice coat of lipstick?

As the Holy Spirit reveals any moments of disobedience, ask God to forgive you. He wants to very much. He is just waiting on you to ask.

Prayer of Reflection

Sovereign Lord, I confess there have been times when I was disobedient to something I felt you telling me to do. (List specific situations the Holy Spirit has brought to mind.) I am sorry for not being obedient or delaying when I should have responded with an immediate yes. Please forgive me and help me to quickly obey when you give me new opportunities. I want to be your obedient daughter because I love you and delight in you. In Jesus' name, amen.

Chapter 4

⚬

Where Can I Go?

(Scripture: Psalm 139)

In the summer of 2021, my husband and I celebrated our 27th wedding anniversary with a trip to the beach. There was just one tiny problem: I didn't exactly do the best research when I booked the spot. I just followed the suggestion of a friend who said her family loved the town.

So, we set out for our destination. . . and drove and drove and drove.

It was a lot farther than I had realized, but in my defense, it didn't look that far on the map. Thankfully, when we arrived at our cute condo close to the beach, we realized it was worth the extra effort, until it was time to come home and the drive loomed in front of us again.

Getting Away

What comes to your mind when you think of a getaway? Beaches? Mountains? A bustling city or rolling countryside?

For me, the word *getaway* brings thoughts of rest and reading, time to be still in the presence of God, conversations with loved ones, and peaceful moments to restore and rejuvenate.

I wonder if Jonah's getaway had even a moment of peace.

When we left him, he was sailing on the deep blue sea, heading as far away from Nineveh and God's call as he could get. Remember what Scripture said:

> But Jonah got up to run away from the Lord by going to Tarshish. He went to the city of Joppa, where he found a ship that was going to the city of Tarshish. Jonah paid for the trip and went aboard, planning to go to Tarshish to run away from the Lord. (Jonah 1:3)

Jonah was intent on running away from God. Think about that for a minute. Exactly how far would be enough distance to achieve that goal? How did Jonah think he could get away from God's will, much less from God himself?

Where Can I Run from You?

Jonah wasn't the first person in Scripture to think about God's presence. Psalm 139 records the words of David, the poet-king, as he marvels at the fact there's not anywhere he could go where God would not be. As an Israelite, Jonah would have been very familiar with King David, the second king of Israel and one who was to be the forebearer (ancestor) of the promised Messiah. Since we may not share Jonah's background knowledge, it may help to know David was the youngest son of a man named Jesse. While still a boy, he was the shepherd for his father's flocks. One day, while checking on his brothers in the king's army, that shepherd boy took on a giant named Goliath who had ridiculed God and his people (1 Samuel 17). David had been anointed king at an early age by the prophet Samuel, but trusted God with the timing. King Saul, who was Israel's first king, became jealous of David and tried to kill him repeatedly. Yet, David served God faithfully, even refusing to kill King Saul when he had the chance (1 Samuel 24).

David was also a poet, and many of his writings are collected in the book of Psalms. In Psalm 139, the poet-king wrestled with questions that were about to become very relevant for Jonah:

> Where can I go to get away from your spirit?
> Where can I run from you?

> If I go up to the heavens, you are there; If I lie down in the grave, you are there.

> If I rise with the sun in the east and settle in the west beyond the sea,

> even there you would guide me. With your right hand you would hold me.

> I could say, "The darkness will hide me. Let the light around me turn into night."

> But even the darkness is not dark to you. The

night is as the day; darkness and light are the same to you. (Psalm 139:7-12)

The psalmist poetically described what theologians call God's omnipresence. The *International Standard Bible Encyclopedia* explains the term as follows:

> Neither the noun "omnipresence" nor adjective "omnipresent" occurs in Scripture, but the idea that God is everywhere present is throughout presupposed and sometimes explicitly formulated. God's omnipresence is closely related to His omnipotence and omniscience: that He is everywhere enables Him to act everywhere and to know all things, and, conversely, through omnipotent action and omniscient knowledge He has access to all places and all secrets (compare Psalm 139). Thus conceived, the attribute is but the correlate of the monotheistic conception of God as the Infinite Creator, Preserver and Governor of the universe, immanent in His works as well as transcendent above them.[21]

I don't know about you, but that last sentence threw me a bit: "Thus conceived, the attribute is but the correlate of the monotheistic conception of God as the Infinite Creator, Preserver and Governor of the universe, immanent in His works as well as transcendent above them." Let's look at the amazing truth packed into those words.

God's omnipresence is a key connection (the correlate) in our understanding of the one true God. Monotheism, or having only one

God, is central to the Christian faith just as it was to the covenant God established with the Israelites. "You must not have any other gods except me" (Exodus 20:3) was the first commandment given to Moses when God established how the Israelites were to relate to him. So, omnipresence helps us understand more about the incredible God we worship. He made, keeps, and rules creation—the whole universe as this definition. He exists within creation, spread through every part of it (is immanent), and at the same time, being well beyond and above our normal physical experience (is transcendent). God is not bound by time or space.

With that expanded definition in mind, let's recall what David said. It doesn't matter how high or low we go, how far east or west, whether we seek out darkness or step into the light, God will still be wherever we are. His presence is everywhere.

Perhaps the most tangible experience I had with this truth was on the night my daddy died. My sister had called at 3:15 a.m. letting me know he was gone. It was the darkest part of the night, and I felt a vast emptiness stretching before me when I thought about our great loss. One of my first thoughts after I ended the call was that I didn't have an earthly father who loved me anymore.

I grabbed some clothes, told my husband through thick tears I would meet him at my parents' house as soon as he could get there, and stumbled out into the night. I locked our front door and turned to make my way to my car in the driveway.

There, spread across the sky were the brightest stars I had ever seen. The September sky was clear, and it looked like I could reach out and touch the heavens. My heart was flooded with peace. Gazing into that sky, I knew beyond a shadow of a doubt that while my earthly father was gone, I had a heavenly Father who loved me and who saw me in my darkest moment.

The loss was still difficult, but I did not have to walk the valley alone because God was with me. Amid my grief, my heart could cry out with praise for my Creator and Sustainer who was with me through the pain.

That moment reminded me of a profound truth: God is everywhere we could ever go, even through the valley of the shadow of death as Psalm 23 tells us. How does that knowledge make you feel? Your response may well depend on your thoughts about God.

God's Omnipresence is Comforting

A.W. Tozer, an American pastor and author of the early-to-mid-20th century, wrote, "What comes into our minds when we think about God is the most important thing about us."[22]

Our reaction to the knowledge of God's omnipresence depends on our relationship with him and our understanding of who he is. If we think he is a cosmic killjoy wanting to keep us in line, we may wish for darkness deep enough to hide us. If we think he is only a judge ready to catch us in wrongdoing, we may long for a cave deep enough to hide us.

If we understand God's great love for us, then we are free to trust him and invite him into the dark places inside our heart. Oh dear friend, the fact we serve a God who can see in the darkness means he can see us in the deepest, most painful moments of our lives.

But if we understand God's great love for us, then we are free to trust him and invite him into the dark places inside our heart. Oh dear friend, the fact we serve a God who can see in the darkness means he can see us in the deepest, most painful moments of our lives.

When we draw near to God in repentance and faith, we will find it removes separation between us and gives us perfect fellowship with God. He is all-powerful. He shaped our world and the entire universe with his Word. He loves us completely and invites us to be his daughters. Through faith in Jesus, we can call God *Abba Father*, which is close to the idea of *Daddy*.

Look at Psalm 139:17. Here, David celebrates an intimate relationship with God, and we begin to realize he was comforted by the knowledge of God's presence wherever he might go.

> "God, Your thoughts are precious to me. They are so many!"

Scripture tells us David had a special relationship with God. 1 Samuel 13:14 records the moment when the prophet Samuel tells Israel's first king, Saul, he had lost the Lord's blessing.

> "But now your kingdom must end, for the Lord has sought out a man after his own heart" (NLT).

A man after God's own heart. That man was David.

> But God removed Saul and replaced him with David, a man about whom God said, "I have found David son of Jesse, a man after my own heart. He will do everything I want him to do" (Acts 13:22 NLT).

I don't know about you, but I want to understand more about a person God described as "a man after my own heart." It wasn't just something people said about him. This verse in Acts makes it clear this was God's view of David. We don't have time to look at all the ways David reflected God's heart, but one of them directly intersects—and contrasts—with Jonah's story.

David found God's knowledge of him precious. This word means something "of great value, not to be wasted or treated carelessly."[23] It might help with our understanding of this definition if we think along the lines of precious gems. To David, the fact God was everywhere and could see him regardless of where he was became a comforting thought. He held this truth close to his heart and counted it among his greatest treasures.

And keep in mind, he was a king who had a lot of treasures.

Drawing Closer Still

David not only rejoiced in this truth that God was near; he invited God even closer. Look at his prayer at the end of this Psalm:

> God, examine me and know my heart; test me
> and know my nervous thoughts.
>
> See if there is any bad thing in me. Lead me on
> the road to everlasting life. (Psalm 139:23-24)

David's heart cried out for God to carefully examine his whole being, to test him and offer correction as needed. He opened his life before the Lord and invited him to examine it. David wanted to remove anything that would keep him separated from God.

In John 10:10a, Jesus warns that we have a very real Enemy who wants to steal, kill, and destroy. One of the things he most wants to steal is our intimacy with God. He wants to convince us darkness and distance are where we thrive; but if we follow this path, it leads to death. Our spiritual death.

God invites us into something much greater. It's right there in the second half of John 10:10,

> "The thief's purpose is to steal and kill and destroy. My purpose is to give them a rich and satisfying life."

Though he lived well before the promises of the New Testament, David understood God was inviting him into something precious, something personal, and something powerful: relationship with the Almighty God. And that relationship was, as relationship with God always is, rooted in our obedience. David drew closer to God because of this incredible calling.

Jonah's response was so different. He wanted to get away. To escape. To hide.

But he was about to find out just how hard it was to flee from the Lord.

What about us? What do we feel when we think of God's omnipresence? Does it seem irrelevant to your life? Is it scary to think he knows you so intimately? Or do you, like David, find this truth comforting?

Dive Deeper

Journal what it means to know you can't get away from God's presence.

Are you more like David or Jonah? Does the thought of God knowing you completely make you uncomfortable or frightened? Does it bring you comfort? Spend a few moments talking with God about your answer and asking him to show you the beauty of always being in his presence.

Claim the promise of James 4:8: "Come near to God, and God will come near to you." Prayerfully consider what practical steps you can take to draw closer to God. Consider the importance of spending time reading and studying God's Word, praying, and being part of a church community and small group. Ask the Lord how you can use your unique gifts and talents to honor him and pray for opportunities to share your faith with others. Ask him to forgive any sins he brings to mind.

Prayer of Reflection

Holy God, give me a heart like David's so I will be a person after your heart. I am glad you see me and know me completely. Lord, please draw near to me. Examine my heart and my thoughts. Reveal to me anything unholy in my life and any offensive way I have. Jesus, thank you for paying the price for my sins. Please cleanse me with your blood. Thank you for forgiving my sins and clothing me in Christ's righteousness. In your precious name, Jesus, I pray, amen.

Chapter 5

⤢

The Flight

(Scripture: Jonah 1 and 2)

Have you ever watched a toddler who thinks he got away with something his parents told him not to do? He's running as fast as his little legs can carry him away from the one who loves him and wants what is best for him. He's probably laughing, giddy with delight at having made his escape. Until, of course, he stumbles over a twig, a corner of a rug, or maybe his own two feet. The laughter is instantly transformed as he tumbles to the ground. From there, he cries out for the very one he was trying to escape.

Jonah has a lot in common with that toddler.

We left Jonah doing his best to get as far away from Nineveh and God's call as he could. And then we reach verse 4.

> "But the Lord sent a great wind on the sea,
> which made the sea so stormy that the ship was
> in danger of breaking apart" (Jonah 1:4).

Those deep blue waters that had looked like such an appealing escape route now looked like a watery grave. The introductory notes to the book of Jonah in *The Devotional Bible* by Max Lucado point out key themes for Jonah. Number two on the list is "God is more powerful than our schemes and plans."[24]

Jonah found this out the hard way. Like our wayward toddler, he's down, and he knows it.

Disobedience Has Unintended Consequences

Jonah wasn't the only person affected by his disobedience. He put the people on the boat with him at risk too. They show up for the first time in verse 5, scared and praying to all the gods they could think of, desperately asking for help. They threw everything that wasn't nailed down into the sea, trying to lighten the load. They possibly even threw in a few nailed down things too, just for good measure.

Someone must have missed Jonah. Maybe they asked, *"Hey, where's that guy we picked up for the trip? He didn't get thrown overboard, did he?"*

The captain went below to check and found him.

But unlike the rest of them, Jonah was not frightened, and he wasn't praying. He wasn't trying to lighten the load. He wasn't lifting a finger to try and save them all.

Nope.

Not a finger.

What was he doing instead?

Snoring away.

Okay, so the Bible doesn't actually say he was snoring, but it does mention he'd gone way down inside the ship and was "fast asleep" (Jonah 1:5).

The captain wasn't pleased.

I don't know a lot about ship captains of the mid-700s BC, but I've seen enough of the stereotype portrayed on TV and in the movies to picture how the scene might have happened. Jonah was sound asleep, and the captain, who was probably used to being in control, had finally found something he could fix.

"Get up, man!" he might have yelled, possibly with a few extra words thrown in to make his point. Verse 6 tells us he asked Jonah why he was sleeping and then told him to pray, to ask whoever Jonah's god was for help in case he might be able to make a difference. The captain used the lowercase g on god, not knowing Jonah served the God of Israel, the true God, the Lord God Almighty.

And he certainly didn't know Jonah's disobedience to God was the cause of all their trouble. They learn this in verse 7 when they try to figure out the problem. God used the casting of lots to reveal the truth. What did they discover? It was Jonah's fault.

They wanted to understand. Verse 8 tells us they asked Jonah questions. I wonder if they all asked them at the same time, if their questions swirled around the deck like waves and rain thrown by the wind.

"Who caused our trouble?"

"What's your job?"

"Where are you from?"

"Who are your people?"

Jonah answered their questions, telling them he was a Hebrew and adding "I fear the Lord, the God of heaven, who made the sea and the land" (Jonah 1:9).

The Bible tells us in verse 10 the men were terrified. Apparently, Jonah told them he was running from God, and they wanted to know what he'd done and what they were supposed to do with him.

Jonah gave them the answer.

"Throw me into the sea."

His words amount to something like, *"I told God I'd rather die than obey him, so let's make it happen. Just toss me into the sea, and this whole thing will be over. You'll be safe, and I'll be dead. And this will be the best thing."*

Because he decided he would rather die than obey.

Here, the sailors provide an ironic contrast to God's wayward prophet.

On the one hand, we have Jonah, this prophet of Israel who wasn't willing to preach to Nineveh because he didn't want them to be forgiven. He wanted to see them punished. On the other hand, we have a group of pagan sailors. They were praying to all kinds of gods and seemingly didn't know the one true God. Yet they didn't want to see the guilty punished. They didn't want to be part of taking this man's life, even though it seemed to be part of God's plan.

So, they did what sailors do. They did what we all do sometimes. They tried to work out the problem in their own strength. They started to row and fight against the storm, trying to move themselves toward shore. "But they could not, because the sea was becoming more stormy" (Jonah 1:13).

Have you ever rowed against a problem in your own power and gotten nowhere? I slipped into this self-reliance habit not too long ago at work. I had a week of vacation coming up, and my to-do list had grown exponentially. Like those sailors chunking needed supplies into the sea, I tried harder and determined to work longer hours, however many it took, to accomplish all the tasks before me. I struggled and wound up frustrated and exhausted. I frantically worked in my own strength, placing my trust in my abilities without inviting God into the process. I wanted to control my circumstances and was striving hard but only wearing myself out because I was trusting in my strength. God wants better for us than that. He wants us to trust Him, to invite Him into our days, our work, and even our to-do lists. I surrendered and released the white-knuckled grip I had on my situation. I asked God to forgive my self-reliance – again – and to guide me in what He wanted me to focus on. The work still remained in front of me, but I was now resting in God's peace rather than in the whirlwind of my own making. The wind and waves of deadlines and checklists returned to their normal size, and I could see how to move forward with peace and grace, for myself and others.

After all else had failed them, verses 14 and 15 tell us, the sailors realized they had no choice but to do what Jonah had suggested and to hurl him into the sea. They prayed God would not count them as guilty. Then? They tossed Jonah overboard.

Picture the scene from their point of view. The waves slapped the boat, threatening to push *them* overboard. The wind stung their faces. The sky was dark and raging. They laid their hands on Jonah, prayers still on their lips for God's forgiveness, and they flung him over the side of the ship.

What was it like for the sailors during his dramatic fall from the deck to the sea? Did they regret their lack of a better choice? Jonah disappeared into the dark waters, and the furious sea became calm (Jonah 1:15).

Just like a switch had been flipped.

The boat no longer rocked, the wind and waves were still, and I imagine the moonlight glinted on the water. I picture them, their eyes fixed on where Jonah went under. Perhaps they stared for a long moment, realizing what had just happened. They encountered God.

Verse 16 says "they began to fear the Lord very much." They made a sacrifice and made promises to God. They'd been changed by the encounter with God's prophet,

who was

at that very moment

sinking

and sinking

under the sea.

Into the Water

The human mind has a great capacity for processing information. A quick Google search found studies saying the amount of information we process ranges from 400 billion bits of information per second to 11 million bits from our bodies alone[25] to only sixty bits according to a 2009 study.[26] Even using the lowest of those numbers (and let's do because it's hard to wrap our minds around numbers like 400 billion and 11 million, but we know what sixty looks like), it is still a lot of information crammed into one second. "One Mississippi" or however you learned to count seconds is not a lot of time, but even sixty bits of information is a lot of input.

I wonder how many seconds it took from when Jonah realized the sailors were going to throw him into the sea before he reached the water.

Five? Ten? Sixty? More?

What did he see? What did he feel? What information was his brain processing?

I'm guessing there was fear, maybe tinged with regret. Maybe his mind was so consumed by his anger all he could think was, *Yep, I'd rather die than go to Nineveh. So, here we go. I'm going to die.*

One Mississippi. Two Mississippi.

I can't help but believe his brain likely noted the storm, those waves and winds and the stinging rain. Was there thunder? I would imagine so, with bright flashes of lightning to go along with the heavy booms.

Three Mississippi. Four Mississippi.

I wonder if Jonah looked at the faces of the sailors and thought about the danger he'd put them in, or if he believed those were the last faces he'd ever see.

Five Mississippi. Six Mississippi.

How high was the deck from which he was thrown? Did he have far to fall or did the craft sit lower in the water? However far, he surely knew he was going down into the angry sea.

Seven Mississippi. Eight Mississippi.

Then there's the touch of the water. Was it shockingly cold, or was Jonah already chilled from the wind and rain?

Nine Mississippi. Ten Mississippi.

Was there a splash with Jonah sliding into the water, or did the fish snatch him from the air?

Eleven Mississippi. Twelve Mississippi.

Did he feel the difference when the storm calmed? Did he have time to think maybe, just maybe, he'd got something right with this last act as he had given up his life to save the crew? Did he think something like, *At least, the guys on the ship will be safe. At least, their deaths won't be on my head. Unlike those folks in Nineveh.*

Thirteen Mississippi. Fourteen Mississippi.

At least I can die in peace.

And then something changed. Suddenly the sinking sensation was gone, and the water subsided. God, it would seem, was not finished with his prophet.

Chapter 1 ends with, "the Lord caused a big fish to swallow Jonah, and Jonah was inside the fish three days and three nights" (Jonah 1:17).

God wanted to write the rest of this amazing adventure, and he wanted Jonah alive for it. Some commentators have suggested Jonah survived in the belly of the fish while others reason he may have been in the recesses of the fish's mouth. While the specifics of the accommodating fish anatomy aren't included, it is clear God was giving Jonah another chance. He wanted Jonah to be the one to carry out his plan to reach the people of Nineveh.

I don't know why God chose Jonah. I don't know why God uses me either, but I'm glad he does.

I wonder how Jonah felt when the drowning sensations left his body.

Had he seen the big fish coming? Did he wonder if being digested by a fish would hurt worse than the pain of drowning—which maybe he already had been thinking about, if not feeling?

I wonder how soon after the fish swallowed Jonah he realized he wasn't going to drown and his life wasn't over.

Some months ago, the national news had the story of a man who was diving for lobsters near Cape Cod when he was scooped up into the mouth of a humpback whale. He described sudden darkness and feeling as if he'd run into a wall. He was inside the whale's mouth for only thirty seconds or so but recounted how he thought something like, *This is it. This is how I die.* His said this thoughts then turned to his family and how he would likely never see them again.

Did Jonah think of his family? Did he mourn a future now seemingly lost at sea?

Fish Thoughts

In chapter 4 of this book, we looked at Psalm 139 where David wrote about the presence of the Lord. He asked the questions, "Where can I go from your Spirit? Where can I flee from your presence?" (Psalm 139:7). Verse 8b adds, "If I make my bed in the depths, you are there."

I wonder if those words swirled around Jonah along with the seaweed and food and muck that may have been with him inside the fish. Jonah had been so committed to his flight plan he had been hurled into the sea rather than submitting to God's call on his life.

He thought he had the final word.

Now, here he was in what I can only imagine was a dark and (most likely) stinky place, realizing David was right. God was still present, and he was still God. He still controlled even the digestive systems of fish, creating a holding cell for a disobedient prophet he wanted to give another chance just as much as he wanted to give to the people of Nineveh.

> Jonah was inside the fish for three days and three nights (Jonah 1:17).

What did Jonah think about during those seventy-two hours? Had he passed out from the trauma of thinking he was dead? Did he wake to find it hard to move because of the seaweed wrapped around his head and arms? Was he exhausted from his flight and his plight?

Was he able to sleep in the belly of the fish like he'd done in the belly of the ship which might have been sailing above him, moving away from the traumatic scene on the now calm sea?

Or was Jonah fully conscious, completely aware of his situation? Did he marvel as he took a first tentative, choking breath filled with the stench of fish insides, wondering how he could breathe under the sea? Did his eyes adjust, or were those seemingly endless hours spent in complete and utter darkness?

Did he hear Satan (also known as the Accuser or Father of Lies) whispering he no longer had the right to pray? Was he reminded that his sin and disobedience had landed him in this deep, dark pit and it was exactly where he deserved to stay? Did despair make its bed alongside him with the fish guts?

Time passed slowly, I imagine. But finally, Jonah began to pray. Chapter 2 of Jonah records his prayer, prayed from "inside the fish":

When I was in danger,

I called to the Lord,

and he answered me.

I was about to die,

so I cried to you,

and you heard my voice.

You threw me into the sea,

down, down into the deep sea.

The water was all around me,

and your powerful waves flowed over me.

I said, "I was driven out of your presence,

but I hope to see your Holy Temple again."

The waters of the sea closed around my throat.

The deep sea was all around me;

seaweed was wrapped around my head.

When I went down to where the mountains of
the sea start to rise,

I thought I was locked in this prison forever,

but you saved me from the pit of death,

Lord, my God.

When my life had almost gone,

I remembered the Lord.

I prayed to you,

and you heard my prayers in your Holy Temple.

People who worship useless idols

give up their loyalty to you.

But I will praise and thank you

while I give sacrifices to you,

and I will keep my promises to you.

Salvation comes from the Lord!

Did you hear the words, prayed from the belly of the fish?
"I hope."
"You saved me."
"I remembered the Lord. I prayed to you."
"And you heard."
God had saved Jonah from drowning and let him live. And
there, inside the fish, Jonah dared to hope. He dreamed of seeing
God's temple—of worshiping the Lord again. He wanted a restored
relationship with God. And he needed to confess his disobedience.

Like Jonah, we need to admit when we have disobeyed. We first
admit our identity as a sinner, and second, we tell God about our
specific sins. He already knows, but when we name our sins to him,

apologize for them, and ask for forgiveness in the name of Jesus, we receive God's forgiveness.

*Like Jonah, we need to admit when we have disobeyed.
We first admit our identity as a sinner,
and second, we tell God about our specific sins.
He already knows, but when we name our sins to him,
apologize for them, and ask for forgiveness
in the name of Jesus, we receive God's forgiveness.*

God forgave Jonah, and he immediately praised and thanked God. Note that Jonah proclaimed God's salvation while he was still inside the fish. He surely realized God had preserved his life in this most unusual way. While in the middle of those desperate circumstances, Jonah praised God for salvation, and verse 10 tells us, Jonah found himself spit out on dry land.

Scripture doesn't record Jonah's condition after being tossed into the sea and swallowed by a fish, but I imagine he was less than April-fresh. My mind's eye pictures him with seaweed and fish slime still clinging to him, shocked he's once again seeing the light of day.

Jonah praised God while he was still inside the fish. This behavior may seem strange to some, but faith in God gives us hope so we can praise God and thank him even during overwhelming circumstances.

In the summer of 2018, I was diagnosed with breast cancer. It was operable and completely survivable, but still a frightening diagnosis and a long journey through tests, surgery, and radiation. But through every moment, inside scary waiting rooms and a loud, uncomfortable MRI machine, God made his presence known. My heart echoed with the Deuteronomy 31:6 promise that God would never leave me nor forsake me. I learned anew I could praise him even in those frightening moments.

Just over a year later, my brother was diagnosed with pancreatic cancer. The prognosis was bleak; his cancer was terminal. He moved back home to be with our mom and sister as he navigated chemo which would, at best, add weeks or months to his life. And in those dark moments, inside the belly of what could have been despair, I saw his faith. One particularly heart-wrenching moment was when he (completely bedridden by the ravages of his cancer) drew shallow breaths to sing along to the hymn "How Great Thou Art." He struggled to praise God with breaths difficult for him to draw. He fixed his faith and hope on the promise Jesus had a glorious day with the Son of heaven waiting for him.

Jonah was delivered in this life; my brother was delivered into eternal hope in Heaven with Jesus.

Oh precious friend, rest assured, if we put our faith in Jesus, there is always hope. We can look for hope and praise him, calling on his great name, even while we are still inside the great fish of our circumstances.

Dive Deeper

How does the dramatic scene of the sailors in the storm make you feel? What do you think you would have felt or said had you been one of the sailors?

What about Jonah's choice? Why do you think he told the sailors to throw him into the sea? What do you imagine he was feeling in those moments?

What do you think you would focus on if you were facing your last seconds of life? Thank God for the good things in your life, and if regrets come to mind, pray and ask him what he would have you do about them?

What do you think about the fact Jonah praised God and thanked him for salvation while still inside the great fish?

Prayer of Reflection

Creator God, you spoke the world into existence and you are sovereign over all things, including the raging sea and storms in our lives. Help us be obedient to you, Lord. Thank you for writing Jonah's story so we could see him claiming the promise of returning to your sanctuary, to your presence in the middle of what seemed like hopeless circumstances. Lord, help us to remember your grace, mercy, and love can and will sustain us even in the darkest, scariest moments of our lives. Help us fix our eyes on you Jesus, as the author and finisher of our faith. Thank you for the fresh chances you have given me. I am so thankful for the promise your mercies are new every morning (Lamentations 3:22-23). Thank you for surprising me with how you deliver me from tough situations, using things and people I would have never imagined. Your grace is truly amazing, and I am so thankful you don't give me what I deserve. In Jesus' name, amen.

Chapter 6

⧊

I'll Go...

(Scripture: Jonah 3:1-5)

The scene is so familiar it has become a staple of writers everywhere. A person finds themselves in trouble and calls on the Lord, asking for help. In the crucible of the moment, they are willing to do anything. They promise God they will be different.

A soldier hoping to survive a brutal firefight promises to give up a bad habit. "I'll do anything, God."

A mother watching over her child who's been injured in a car wreck, pledges to be more devoted. "I'll do anything, God."

The film stereotype suggests the pledged change may not last long after the bullets stop flying or the recovery happens. The guaranteed change in behavior made under the pressure of distress is soon forgotten once the crisis has passed.

The question on our minds as we turn to Chapter 3 of Jonah and find our seaweed-covered, stinky prophet coughed up on dry land is whether his change will survive in the light of day. His prayer from the belly of the fish said he would keep his promises to God—but will he now?

The Ninevites haven't changed.

The animosity between the Ninevites and the people of Israel hasn't changed.

The question is: has Jonah changed?

> "The Lord spoke his word to Jonah again and said, "Get up, go to the great city Nineveh, and preach to it what I tell you to say." (Jonah 3:1)

This part of the book happens rather quickly. Just a handful of words capture the pivotal moment in Jonah 3:1-2, but it's a place worth stopping. It's a moment of grace and choice.

If God were like me, he might have raged against Jonah and told him he could never trust him again. If God were like me, he might have held a grudge or simply told Jonah, "You had your chance."

Thank God he's not like me. I mean, I would've left the guy in the fish. Or worse.

Lamentations 3:22-23 tells us God is different. "The Lord's love never ends; his mercies never stop. They are new every morning; Lord, your loyalty is great." Other translations say faithfulness rather than loyalty.

Love and mercy are available each day of our lives; we need only accept them. How do we do that?

1 John 1:9 says, "But if we confess our sins, he will forgive our sins, because we can trust God to do what is right. He will cleanse us from all the wrongs we have done."

The God of the universe will make us completely clean. We
need only to admit we are sinful and in need of his help.
When we ask for forgiveness in the name of his Son Jesus,
God will forgive us and give us a clean record.

Think about that: the God of the universe will make us
completely clean. We need only to admit we are sinful and in need of
his help. When we ask for forgiveness in the name of his Son Jesus,
God will forgive us and give us a clean record.

That's good news, but there's even more. In other places,
Scripture tells us that God's forgiveness isn't like ours when we
forgive, but don't really forget. God forgives completely. The verse
says, "He has taken our sins away from us as far as the east is from
the west" (Psalm 103:12).

Not only does God offer us mercy, but if we are willing to
confess Jesus as Lord, he forgives our sins, removes them far, far
away from us, and then he forgets the sin. Look at this amazing
promise found in Hebrews 8:12, "I will forgive them for the wicked
things they did, and I will not remember their sins anymore."

The stinky prophet stands on dry ground with a clean slate, and
God tells him again to go preach. We can stand forgiven when we
repent—admit we have sinned, confess the sin to God, and ask him
to make us clean through the blood of Jesus.

The Lord had gotten Jonah's attention and changed his heart, so
Jonah was indeed willing to be obedient. In verse 3 we see a prophet
who is no longer running. He was quick to obey this time.

"So Jonah obeyed the Lord and got up and went
to Nineveh." (Jonah 3:3)

Considering the Inconsiderable

I love looking at pictures of big cities. Bright taillights stream off
into the nighttime. The city glows. One image containing so much
vibrancy almost makes you feel the life teeming within.

But I'm a small-town girl. If you get more than sixty miles away
from here, it's rare anyone has heard of my hometown. There are
smaller places, but my town is a far cry from a New York City, a
Chicago or a Los Angeles.

Jonah was from a small town, too.

The *International Standard Bible Encyclopedia* describes his hometown
as "an inconsiderable village, about two miles from Sepphoris on the
Tiberias road."[27]

Did you catch the word inconsiderable? I looked it up. It means:

"Small, as in value, amount or size,"

"not worth consideration or notice, trivial."

Inconsiderable.[27]

I feel inconsiderable sometimes. I feel insignificant and not
worth consideration. I wonder as a writer what valuable thing I could
possibly have to say. I ask the same question in my friendships and
experiences as just an everyday, ordinary person.

Did Jonah feel any of these things as he approached "the great
city of Nineveh"?

Did he feel like the Israelite version of a country bumpkin? Did
his small-town mannerisms give away his upbringing? Did he stick
out like a sore thumb as he approached the bustling metropolis?

When I think about Nineveh, the word I picture is vast.

Jonah 3:3 tells us it would take a person three days to walk across the city.

Synonyms for vast? "Measureless, boundless, gigantic, colossal, stupendous."[29]

And the opposite? Small.

Inconsiderable.

So, what makes the difference here? What would make this vast city—the one the Lord called "the great city of Nineveh" (Jonah 3:1)—pay attention to a maybe still-stinky prophet from an inconsiderable town?

He came with a message from God and had been sent by God. And God changes our unworthiness. When we put our trust in Jesus as our Savior, He gives us a completely new identity. We're not the same person we were. We now find our identity in him rather than in our small-town roots or our big-city culture.

Whatever reluctance Jonah had about going to Nineveh, whatever hesitancy to preach the message God had given him, he approached the great city.

Jonah had come to town. He walked into the city, headed into the heart of it, and began to preach.

We don't have great sermons recorded in the book of Jonah. A lot of other books about the prophets record word-for-word the messages God gave them to share. But Jonah's message is summed up in seven words.

> "After forty days, Nineveh will be destroyed."
> (Jonah 3:4)

I used to think the brief message meant Jonah didn't bother too much because he hadn't wanted to come in the first place. This is certainly possible, but I also think God's message may have been for the people of Nineveh at their time in history. Perhaps Jonah (or the person telling of his life) wants us to focus on the prophet rather than the message itself.

The book paints a great picture of God's mercy and grace, both to the people of Nineveh and to his unwilling prophet. And his mercy and grace are what we need to focus on.

Whether Jonah's seven words were all he said, the people of Nineveh responded. Verse 5 says simply, "The people of Nineveh believed God." But the truth behind this statement isn't the least bit simple.

The belief, the asking God for forgiveness, is a crucial part of what we are called to do. In the next chapter, we'll dig a little deeper into what "believing God" looked and felt like for the people of Nineveh—and maybe learn what it can feel like for us today.

For now, what about you?

Sit and ponder God's forgiveness. Does the whole idea that God could and would forgive the Ninevites seem too good to be true? That he can and would forgive you? When we put our faith in God through Jesus, he takes our mistakes, bad choices, and willful rebellion and gives us a new beginning as part of his family. Reread the verses shared in this chapter, look them up in different translations, and ask the Holy Spirit to guide you to understand their meaning on a deeper level.

Dive Deeper

What does God's offer of forgiveness mean to you? Spend a few moments reflecting on the verses shared in this chapter and let the Holy Spirit guide you. Confess any sins you recall, and praise the Lord for the deliverance he offers through Jesus.

Have you ever felt inconsiderable? Like you have nothing to offer when it comes to spiritual matters?

What does it mean to you that God uses people from places like Jonah's hometown and the author's hometown? What about God's willingness to use imperfect people like Jonah and like the author?

Prayer of Reflection

Most gracious heavenly Father, thank you for loving us despite our sin. Thank you for making a way through the perfect sacrifice of Jesus' death and resurrection so we can stand forgiven before you. Lord, help us to live in light of this beautiful truth. Thank you for using us when the world says we aren't worth considering. Thank you for using Jonah, and thank you for inviting us into your beautiful plan to tell the world about your great love and offer of forgiveness. Help us find our identity in you and not in who we think we are or where we come from. Remind us when we are covered in the precious blood of Christ's sacrifice on the cross, we stand forgiven before you as dearly loved daughters.

Great is your faithfulness. Thank you for your boundless, unfailing mercy! In Jesus' powerful name we pray, amen.

Chapter 7

∽

Believing God

(Scripture: Jonah 3:5-10)

A few weeks ago, my husband and I went to the historic movie
theatre in our hometown to see the film *Jesus Revolution*,[29] which
chronicles the beginnings of a religious movement that took place
in the 1960s and 70s. I found myself peering back into a time I have
never fully understood, fascinated by the seemingly random hap-
penings—from roadside encounters to passing conversations—that
when viewed through the eyes of faith showed the hand of God at
work.

We'd chosen the film based on the recommendation of others,
and I knew little of what to expect. It took me a while (and some
post-theatre online searching) to realize I was seeing not just the
story of what would become a national movement, but the testimony

of a man who would go on to become a leading pastor influencing generations for the Lord.

But in the film he was just Greg—a young man with emotional scars from a troubled home who found himself with more questions about God than he had answers. There's a pivotal scene where Greg is confronted with the message that God loves him and wants a personal relationship with him through Jesus.

But Greg is scared. He's been let down so many times before. He's tried to find fulfillment in the hippie culture, chasing a feeling (or anything) that would fill the emptiness inside him. In a pivotal scene, he struggles with whether he should choose to trust in Jesus, asking something like, "What if it's just another empty high that fades?" Greg must now decide his path. Will he choose to trust, placing his faith in Jesus as Savior, or will he choose to try to run his life on his own, have his way about things, but still feel empty and hopeless? The movie makes it plain that Greg was faced with a moment when he had to decide.

That moment comes for all of us.

In chapter 3 of the book of Jonah, we see that moment unfolding for the Ninevites.

Jonah has finally been obedient. Now our focus shifts to the Ninevites. Would they heed God's call for repentance? What will they choose to do when they are faced with their moment of decision?

Jonah 3:5 tells us the Ninevites "believed God." They gave up food for a while and put on mourning clothes as an outward symbol of their sorrow for their sin. They were heartbroken at how they'd dishonored God, and they wanted to show it.

Everyone did this together. Rich and poor. Master and servant. From the most important to the least important. A city-wide revival started with the people, but it took a bit of time for the news to reach the king.

Jonah 3:6 simply says the king heard the news. I can't help but wonder what that looked like. Did he hear whispers in the halls of the palace or notice favorite officials suddenly missing from their duties? Were they at home wearing their mourning clothes, feeling bad because of their sin? Did the king ask someone what all the whispering was about, or did he demand their silence and ask what was so important they needed to talk? Did he look out the window of the palace and see the people wearing their sorrow? Did he ask, *"What is wrong with all these people?"* Imagine with me what that might have looked like.

"Well, this prophet came to town. . . "

"A prophet? What kind of prophet? Where was he from? What's some foreign prophet got to do with us?"

"Your Majesty, he was really sort of a stinky fellow. But he talked about the sin of Nineveh and said the city would be destroyed in forty days."

"Forty days? When did this happen?"

"Yesterday? The day before?"

Then the king got up from his throne (those words are written in verse 6) and took off his royal robe. He put on clothes made of rough cloth. He sat in ashes and mourned his sin and his people's sin. He was upset, and he wanted to show it.

He did what kings often do; he issued a decree (verse 7).

No one was to eat or drink water—not people, not animals. Everyone was to put on their mourning clothes. And when they were properly attired, they were to cry out to the Lord.

The king demanded it.

The king hoped it would make a difference.

Jonah 3:8-9 records the rest of his decree: "Everyone must turn away from evil living and stop doing harm all the time. Who knows? Maybe God will change his mind. Maybe he will stop being angry, and then we will not die."

The people of Nineveh and their king got it. They were confronted with their sin, and they took a long, hard look at themselves. Maybe this was the first time they'd heard of the one true God they were sinning against. It's possible this could have been one reason why it became so important for Jonah to share this message with them.

Once they recognized their sin, the people cried out to God. They asked him for forgiveness and turned from their sin. The king described what was needed, saying, "Everyone must turn away from evil living and stop doing harm all the time." (Jonah 3:8b)

What a wonderful description of repentance, turning away from sin and self, and turning to God! The king realized it wasn't enough to simply say they were sorry then continue living any old way. To receive forgiveness from God, a change of heart was required, and they needed to make one fast.

The king hoped it would make a difference. He hoped by leading his people in repentance God would change his mind. It was the only hope they had.

Within the century, another prophet (Isaiah) would write these words: "The Lord says, 'Come, let us talk about these things. Though your sins are like scarlet, they can be as white as snow. Though your sins are deep red, they can be white like wool'" (Isaiah 1:18).

Soon, another prophet named Micah would write,

> There is no God like you. You forgive those who
> are guilty of sin; you don't look at the sins of your

people who are left alive. You will not stay angry forever, because you enjoy being kind. You will have mercy on us again; you will conquer our sins. You will throw away all our sins into the deepest part of the sea. (Micah 7:18-19)

The Ninevites didn't have those lessons to learn from. Unlike us, they certainly didn't have the benefit of the New Testament teachings on how we can have a relationship with God through forgiveness because of the death and resurrection of Jesus. But we do, so let's look at a few of those promises.

1 John 1:9 tells us, "But if we confess our sins, he will forgive our sins, because we can trust God to do what is right. He will cleanse us from all the wrongs we have done."

We can be clean from all of our mistakes, our bad choices, our willful disobedience. Perfectly, fully clean. But how? For that answer, let's look at Acts 3:19. That verse says, "So you must change your hearts and lives! Come back to God, and he will forgive your sins. Then the Lord will send the time of rest."

Come back to God? What if I don't know how? What if I can't find my way? That's the most beautiful part! God knew we wouldn't know the way back to relationship with him and even if we were to find it, we could never get there under our own power. So, he sent Jesus who described himself as "the Way" in John 14:6.

Come back to God? What if I don't know how? What if I can't find my way? That's the most beautiful part! God knew we wouldn't know the way back to relationship with him and even if we were to find it, we could never get there under our own power. So, he sent Jesus who described himself as "the Way" in John 14:6.

The one step required of us is believing in Jesus and asking him to forgive us and be the Lord of our lives. When we take that step, Jesus is ready to respond with open arms and welcome us into God's family forever.

Hebrews 10:17 says, "Then he says: 'Their sins and the evil things they do. I will not remember anymore.'"

And we learn even more from a letter the apostle Paul wrote to the church in a city named Ephesus (part of modern Turkey). "In Christ we are set free by the blood of his death, and so we have forgiveness of sins. How rich is God's grace" (Ephesians 1:7).

The king of Nineveh showed great wisdom as he led his people to repent. Maybe as a sovereign, he understood mercy and grace. I wonder if he had been merciful or if he wished he had been quicker to show mercy. Did he fear he'd be treated the way he might have treated others? Through the teachings of Jonah and the leading of God, the king and the people repented. They showed their sorrow. They turned their backs on their sinful way of life.

Verse 10 tells us, "When God saw what the people did, that they stopped doing evil, he changed his mind and did not do what he had warned. He did not punish them."

They repented, and God forgave.

This beautiful truth is written again and again on the pages of Scripture and in the lives of people who have lived throughout time. God calls us into relationship with him. He wants to restore us. He wants to forgive us. But we have to be willing. We must do our part.

When I gave my life to Christ, I realized I had done wrong things that had separated me from God, who is perfect and holy. Nothing I could do would ever be enough to make up for (the biblical word is atone) my sins. And it didn't matter if my family and friends were already Christians; I needed a relationship with Jesus that was all my own. This relationship had to be completely based on the forgiveness Jesus made possible through his death on the cross. There's nothing I need to or can do to help myself beyond asking Jesus to change my heart and be the Lord of my life.

When I gave my life to Christ, I realized I had done wrong things that had separated me from God, who is perfect and holy. Nothing I could do would ever be enough to make up for (the biblical word is atone) my sins. …I needed a relationship with Jesus that was all my own.

The Bible teaches us God is good and loving, and we can always trust his unchanging character and his faithfulness. We have the entire Bible, both Old and New Testaments, to teach us about God. Let's see how looking at Scripture as a whole helps us understand what is happening in the book of Jonah. Let's ask an important question: why would God send Jonah to preach to the Ninevites? This question is crucial in our story. The reason for God's command to Jonah is exactly the same reason God sent his Son to die for our sins as John 3:16 puts it because he "so loved."

God looked at the wicked city of Nineveh and saw they desperately needed saving. Unlike Jonah, God did not see an evil group needing to be wiped off the face of the earth. He saw people who needed to turn to him. In fact, Romans 3:10 tells us we are all like this. "There is no one who always does what is right, not even one." Romans 5:8 adds, "But God shows his great love for us in this way: Christ died for us while we were still sinners."

Jonah Hints at God's Plan for Redemption

Jonah is an Old Testament foreshadowing of the good news or gospel that will unfold in the New Testament. God wanted to restore a relationship of love with humanity since it's why he created us. He wanted to love and care for us, and in return we would love and worship him. Jonah hints at an important development in this journey of restoration. No longer would God's salvation be available only for the Jewish people. Outsiders—those non-Jews we mentioned earlier—were going to be offered forgiveness of sins as well.

I am ever so grateful because I am one of those outsiders.

The rest of John 3:16 explains this idea, saying, "God loved the world so much that he gave his one and only Son so that *whoever* believes in him may not be lost, but have eternal life" (emphasis mine). In Jonah's time, the "whoever" promises were thought to be only for the Jews; but praise the Lord, we have the rest of Scripture to teach us God's whole plan. Paul wrote in Romans 1:16, "For I am not ashamed of the Good News, because it is the power God uses to save everyone who believes—to save the Jews first and then to save non-Jews."

This was God's plan all along. Galatians 3:8 says, "The Scriptures, telling what would happen in the future, said that God would make the non-Jewish people right through their faith. This good news was told to Abraham beforehand, as the Scripture says,

"'All nations will be blessed through you.'" Verse 7 of this chapter says "the true children of Abraham" are "those who have faith."

But wait, it gets even better. God doesn't merely allow us to have blessings. When we believe in him and put our trust in Jesus Christ to save us from our sins, he welcomes us into his family as dearly loved children. Let's return to J.I. Packer's book "Knowing God" for an explanation of this concept:

> Adoption is the highest privilege of the gospel. The traitor is forgiven, brought in for supper, and given the family name… Adoption is a family idea, conceived in terms of love, and viewing God as father. In adoption, God takes us into His family and fellowship—He establishes us as His children and heirs. Closeness, affection, and generosity are at the heart of the relationship. To be right with God the Judge is a great thing, but to be loved and cared for by God the Father is greater."[31]

This incredible invitation to become sons and daughters of God is open to us. God is offering salvation to Nineveh, to us, and to all the "Ninevites" we might not like in this world. He extends his love and grace to all, but the gift must be accepted.

As Greg Laurie discovered in *Jesus Revolution*, we must decide for ourselves.

The first step on the journey is for each of us to decide whether we believe God is good and we are not. We must recognize our sin and the fact we are separated from the Holy God. We must realize there is nothing we can do to help ourselves escape the punishment our sins have earned us.

From within this dark place, we are called to turn our eyes to Jesus who gave his life to pay the penalty for our sins and who rose again to defeat sin and death once and for all.

Have you decided? or yourself? If you've never entered into a personal relationship with Jesus, I pray you will accept His offer of salvation today.

What Does Accepting Jesus' Offer of Salvation Look Like?

Is repentance a new concept for you? God is holy, perfect, and just. We are not. We are sinful people who cannot live up to God's standards for our life. His standard is holiness. Perfection. Without spiritual blemish. Absolutely just and righteous.

Do those things sound like you?

Well, they didn't sound like me either.

In Romans 6:23, Paul wrote, "the wages of sin is death." That verse literally means that what we have rightly earned with our disobedience is the end of our earthly life and eternal separation from God. That paycheck is coming our way because there's a huge gap between us and the perfect God. Nothing we can ever do will fill this chasm. We face death and eternal separation from God.

Oh, but thank God for Jesus!

He came and lived a perfect, sinless life. He was just and completely holy. Then he died on the cross, thoroughly and willingly becoming our sin so we could have the opportunity to put on his righteousness. He rose again, defeating death and returning to reign at the right hand of the Father in heaven. His death paid the penalty for our sin.

We can use the A-B-Cs to help us understand and remember what we need to do:

A — First we must **admit** we are sinners and ask God's forgiveness

B — Then we **believe** Jesus is God's Son, who died on the cross for our sins and **become** a child of God by receiving Christ.

C — Finally we **confess** Jesus is Lord—and not just the Lord or a lord, but our Lord.

But what does confess mean? There are actually two parts of how this word intersects with our need for God's forgiveness. First, like a person guilty of a crime, we confess by admitting we've done wrong and can't save ourselves. Realizing our only hope comes from Christ, we confess (admit, proclaim, stake our life on) Jesus is Lord and we choose to follow him, wherever he might lead (even if it is to our own Nineveh).

When we give our hearts and lives to Jesus in this way, we become a child of God.

And this leads to great rejoicing in heaven.

If you've never accepted Jesus as your Savior, why not do it today by praying something like this:

> *God in heaven, I admit I am a sinner and cannot be perfect and holy in my own power. Lord, I ask you to forgive me. I believe Jesus is your Son. He died on the cross because he loved me and came to save me from my sins. I receive Jesus as my Savior and today become your daughter. I confess Jesus is Lord of my life, and I praise and thank you for saving me. In his precious name, I pray. Amen.*

Maybe you are already a Jesus follower. You have settled the matter of your salvation and are already part of God's family. Praise God for his deliverance and the fellowship he offers. Will you be obedient enough to ask him to show you what assignment he has for you? Will you obey him even when what he asks doesn't make sense by our earthly understanding? Will you trust him even when it hurts?

Dive Deeper

Read J.I. Packer's passage about adoption into God's family on page 93. What stands out to you most from his description?

Have you accepted the forgiveness and fellowship God offers through Jesus?

Scripture teaches when we call on the name of Jesus and accept him as Savior and Lord he will forgive our sins and cleanse us from all unrighteousness. He will remove the separation between us. What a beautiful promise! But it's a gift we must choose to accept.

If you don't know Jesus as your Savior, ask him to come into your heart and to be the Lord of your life. He loves you and welcomes you into relationship with him. You only need to ask him by praying something like this:

Dear God, I realize I am a sinner, and my sin has separated me from you. I come to you in the name of Jesus who died and rose again to pay for my sins. I ask you to make me new. Please forgive me for my sins and become my Lord and Savior. Help me live a life honoring to you. Teach me what it means to be your daughter. In Jesus' name I pray, amen.

If you are already a Christian, thank God for the beautiful gift of forgiveness you've received. Spend time praising him. In your journal, write a prayer of thanksgiving for the salvation he has made possible through Jesus. Then, ask God to show you the assignment he has planned for you. Ask him to reveal how you can share the good news of his love for the world with others.

Chapter 8

⚜

Rejoicing in Heaven

(Scripture: Luke 15; Jonah 4:1-9)

The excerpt from J.I. Packer's "Knowing God" in the last chapter paints a beautiful picture of what it means to be adopted into the family of God. What does it mean to you to be part of a family? Do you have great memories of growing up in a home filled with love or was your story different?

I was a blessed little girl in this respect, and I'm still blessed to have a loving family who nurtured me. Throughout my life, parents, grandparents, siblings, aunts, and uncles loved me and helped me grow and mature as a person. One of the greatest things my family did was teach me about Jesus. I've already mentioned my parents and sister read the Bible to me.

As I child I also sang hymns with my grandmother while I sat at the yellow Formica table in her kitchen. I sang loudly (and probably off-key) while swinging my still-short legs to the music as she tackled chores. Interestingly enough, I found a similar table via Google. I could order a version of this "mid-century" treasure for only $400, but it wouldn't come with the rich layer of love I found at hers. I'm so thankful for the priceless lessons I learned there as she lived out her faith and told me how the Lord had cared for and sustained her through her life.

My family took the call to share Jesus seriously, and I am forever—eternally—grateful.

This assignment to share Jesus is one all believers have received. The Gospel of Matthew ends with Jesus giving his followers (including us) these instructions: "So go and make followers of all people in the world. Baptize them in the name of the Father and the Son and the Holy Spirit" (Matthew 28:19). The first chapter of the book of Acts records this assignment as the final words Jesus said to his disciples before ascending to heaven: "You will be my witnesses in Jerusalem, in all of Judea, in Samaria, and in every part of the world" (Acts 1:8b). The places named in the verse show we are to tell others about Jesus close by, in our neighborhood, our city, and with our own family. But we aren't to stop there. We're supposed to keep going until the good news about Jesus has reached every part of the world.

This call to tell others is known as "The Great Commission," and it's our first job as Christ-followers. Like Jonah, we must decide: will we be obedient?

This call to tell others is known as "The Great Commission," and it's our first job as Christ-followers. Like Jonah, we must decide: will we be obedient?

What happens if God sends us to difficult people or our very own Ninevites? What happens when those we consider evil repent?

Think back to our earlier discussion of enemies. Who came to mind when you heard that word? Do you believe that person should be offered forgiveness, or would you rather see them get what they deserve?

The beauty of the gospel is that none of us gets what we deserve when we put our trust in Jesus and accept him as our Savior. We read about the wages of sin, which is death and eternal separation from God. That's what we all deserve because of our sinful nature. That includes the Ninevites and the enemy you thought of, but it includes you and me as well.

Scripture teaches us that we are evil too: "There is no one righteous; not even one" (Romans 3:10). We can have a relationship with God because of his grace and mercy. I've heard it said that grace is receiving what we don't deserve, and mercy is not receiving what we do deserve. Those gifts are available to everyone.

The book of Jonah tells us that when the Ninevites heard judgment was coming, they asked for forgiveness and stopped doing evil. That's what we call repentance or turning from sin and self and turning to God.

When anyone asks God for forgiveness, God is ready to respond, and it leads to a celebration beyond our wildest imagination.

When anyone asks God for forgiveness,
God is ready to respond, and it leads to
a celebration beyond our wildest imagination.

We learn this from a lesson Jesus shared one day while he was teaching. He told three stories (also called parables) that help us understand how God feels about people and what happens when they choose to say they are sorry and turn away from their sin to following God. Let's look at Luke 15 as Jesus teaches about these topics through the stories of the lost sheep, the lost coin, and the lost son.

In the first parable, Jesus told about a man who had lost a sheep. The man had ninety-nine more so it was no big deal, right? Wrong. Jesus asked, "Doesn't he leave the ninety-nine in the open country and go after the lost sheep until he finds it? And when he finds it, he joyfully puts it on his shoulders and goes home" (Luke 15:4b-6a NIV).[32] The sheep owner was so happy he called in his friends and neighbors to celebrate the return of the sheep.

This first parable teaches that every person matters to God. He will go in search of the lost sheep. Jesus ended this parable by adding, "I tell you that in the same way there will be more rejoicing in heaven over one sinner who repents than over ninety-nine righteous persons who do not need to repent" (Luke 15:7 NIV).

Rejoicing in heaven.

The second story is similar. A woman has lost a silver coin. It was one of only ten she had, and she needed to find it. She lit all the lights, started sweeping, and (as we'd put it now) decluttering to look everywhere for it. She, too, invited her friends and neighbors to join the celebration when she found it.

Again, Jesus adds, "In the same way, I tell you, there is rejoicing in the presence of the angels of God over one sinner who repents" (Luke 15:10 NIV).

Rejoicing in the presence of the angels of God.

Lastly, Jesus told the story of the lost son. Maybe you've heard this one. The younger son got tired of living under his father's rule and possibly in the shadow of his older brother. He started thinking if only he could go out and make his mark on the world, then he wouldn't have any more problems. These thoughts led him to believe if he could just go ahead and have what was coming to him—what he *deserved* from his father's estate—well, then he'd have a start. He could really be somebody instead of being the second son on a second-rate farm. The thoughts brewed until one day he got up had the nerve to ask his father for his inheritance.

This request was hugely disrespectful. The estate was to pass to the sons following the father's death, but here came the youngest son—who would be the recipient of the smaller share—demanding what he thought was rightfully his. A lot of fathers would have thrown him out. A lot of fathers would have given him a lecture, or worse. But this father divided his wealth and gave it to his sons.

You don't have to be familiar with this particular story from Scripture to guess things aren't going to go well for the youngest son. We've seen it played out in hundreds, if not thousands of movies and books. Maybe we've seen it in the lives of friends or family.

It's possible we've lived it ourselves. We could relate to the parent in the story who watched his son turn away, or maybe we were the rebellious child. Whatever our particular experience, we can almost hear the dark music swelling in the background as the son sets off toward a distant land with all his money burning a hole in his pocket.

The youngest son didn't make it very long before he'd lost everything. It's written in Luke 15:13-14 (NIV), "Not long after that the younger son got together all he had, set off for a distant country and there squandered his wealth in wild living. After he had spent everything, there was a severe famine in that whole country, and he began to be in need."

The son tried to work things out in his own power. He got a job and started feeding pigs. Every day, he would throw out slop to pigs, who hungrily gobbled it all up. Maybe it wasn't very long before he could hardly hear them chomping over the rumbling in his own stomach. He was so hungry, Jesus said, "He longed to fill his stomach with the pods that the pigs were eating, but no one gave him anything" (Luke 15:16, NIV).

There in a stinky pig pen, the son started thinking about home. (Jesus described it as "coming to his senses.") He realized maybe things were not as bad at home as he might've thought. He remembered how his father's servants always had plenty of food to eat. And now, he was starving.

Can you imagine the voices he heard in his head as the Enemy of his soul tried to convince him not to return to his loving father?

They'll never take you back.

You were selfish and greedy and stupid.

You don't deserve to be his son. You don't even deserve to be his servant.

You deserve to die here.

Don't you know he was tired to the bone? I think about the hunger and the tiredness, the shame, guilt, and heartache pressing down on him. He had to have felt undeserving, but he wanted so badly to go home.

I felt this same way when I realized I was a sinner separated from God. Nothing I could do would help me. My parents' strong faith wouldn't save me. I needed a relationship with God on my own. I felt uneasy and almost sick as I looked at the hopelessness of my circumstance. And then I realized my only hope was coming home to the Father by asking Jesus to be my Savior. I gave God my shame and guilt, and in return I received salvation, peace, and the right to be called his daughter.

The lost son was about to experience this for himself because he finally made a good choice.

"'I will set out and go back to my father and say to him, "Father, I have sinned against heaven and against you. I am no longer worthy to be called your son; make me like one of your hired servants." So he got up and went to his father'" (Luke 15:18-20, NIV).

And what happened? As he got close to home the father saw him and ran out to meet him (verse 20).

The father had been watching. He had been hoping. He had been ready to rejoice, just like the angels in heaven, for "this son of mine was dead and is alive again; he was lost and is found" (Luke 15:24, NIV).

These three parables show there's great rejoicing in heaven over one person who accepts Christ as their Savior, over each one of those who gives their hearts to him. Consider how great the rejoicing was in heaven over the people of Nineveh. An entire city, young and old, rich and poor, male and female, turned to the Lord. Can you imagine the celebration in heaven? The angels would have sung loud praises to Jesus. Those gathered around the heavenly throne would have shouted, "Hosanna! Hosanna! Worthy is the Lamb (Jesus)!"

There would have been great rejoicing because the one who was lost now is found.

But the story's not quite over, not for the prodigal son's family. And Jonah's adventure isn't over either.

Not Everyone Rejoices

While heaven rang loudly with praise and the father rejoiced in the story of the lost son in Luke 15, there was another person in Jesus' parable: the older brother. We're going to discover he is a lot like Jonah.

The older brother was the good son; he would want to be sure you know that. He was not the one who asked his father for his inheritance, although he had received his as well. Even as the lost son was approaching their homestead, the older brother was working in the field. He was probably hot and tired. He had likely been fed up with his spoiled younger brother for a long time.

As he headed in from the long workday and got close to home, he heard something unusual. *Was that music? Is someone having a party?* He was curious.

See, his dad had been sad. *It broke his heart when my good-for-nothing brother left,* the older brother may have thought. *Dad certainly hadn't been feeling like throwing a party. What in the world is going on?*

He called a servant over to find out.

He got an answer he didn't expect.

"Your brother has come," the servant replied. "And your father has killed the fattened calf because he has him back safe and sound" (Luke 15:27 NIV).

"Excuse me. What? What did you say?" he may have asked.

"Your brother is back. . . " Perhaps the servant's voice trailed off when he saw the look on his young master's face.

Then "the older brother became angry" (Luke 15:28 NIV).

It's easy to picture him raging with words like, "Back? Who does he think he is to come back? I bet he's blown through all the money Dad gave him and came back here thinking he'll get more. He'll never get a dime of my money."

I imagine him pacing, maybe pounding his fist against his hand or at least wanting to with every fiber of his being. He may have even been talking to himself by now, the servant perhaps having retreated to a safe distance in case the rage came in his direction.

The older brother was not happy and certainly wasn't ready to celebrate. But let's see what Jesus is teaching us about their father who represents God the Father. What is he up to while his oldest son is upset? The father had been watching for his lost son and ran to meet him while he was still a long way off. But he hadn't forgotten his older son. He saw this son and wanted his eldest to join the celebration, to share his joy at the return of his youngest son.

The father invited the older brother in.

"I'm not going in there. No way. Nope. Not a chance," may have been the response.

Rather than throwing up his hands in frustration (like I might want to do), the father went out to talk with his son. He wanted his oldest son to understand so the "father went out and pleaded with him" (Luke 15:28 NIV).

But the oldest son was mad. How could the father forgive this younger brother who'd hurt them so much, who'd never respected their family and had thrown away his inheritance?

He answered his father, "Look! All these years I've been slaving for you and never disobeyed your orders. Yet you never gave me even a young goat so I could celebrate with *my* friends. But when *this son of yours* who has squandered your property with prostitutes comes home, you kill the fattened calf for him!" (Luke 15:29-30 NIV, emphasis mine).

Do you hear his heart crying? *I've been the good one. I've worked hard. I've never done wrong. And you know, Dad, you know the kinds of things we heard he's been up to. Remember? What are you doing?*

Imagine the love which must have been visible on the father's face. I picture him laying his aged hand on his son's shoulder giving it a squeeze.

"'My son,' the father said, 'you are always with me, and everything I have is yours. But we had to celebrate and be glad, because this brother of yours was dead and is alive again; he was lost and is found'" (Luke 15:31-32, NIV).

Jesus ended his parable there. We don't get to hear how the brother responded. I believe this might be because Jesus wanted to leave the question open for his listeners, so they could ask themselves how they would respond. Would we, like the older brother, storm about and sulk because the younger brother repented?

Jonah sure did.

He'd gone and preached to the people of Nineveh. He'd made it pretty plain to God he didn't want to. He'd tried to run away because he knew *those* people didn't deserve to hear about God's love. They'd been disrespectful. They'd hurt others (including God's people, meaning the Israelites) with their actions. They didn't deserve the Father's love. But God, like the father in Jesus' parable, was watching for the first sign they wanted to come home and ask forgiveness.

Like the older brother, Jonah didn't like it one bit.

Jonah 4:1 sums it up clearly, "But this (God forgiving the Ninevites) made Jonah very unhappy, and he became angry."

He didn't like it, and he wanted to be sure God knew why.

"He prayed to the Lord, 'When I was still in my own country this is what I said would happen and that is why I quickly ran to Tarshish. I knew that you are a God who is kind and shows mercy. You don't become angry quickly, and you have great love. I knew you would choose not to cause harm'" (Jonah 4:2).

In our modern words he told God, *"See, God. I told you so. I knew you'd do this! This is why I ran. I didn't want any part of it, and we are exactly where I knew we'd wind up."*

Then Jonah returned to his familiar theme of: "I'd rather die than be part of this." He says that right in Jonah 4:3.

> "So now I ask you, Lord, please kill me. It is better for me to die than to live."

Jonah's words seem ironic for a guy who had been given a second chance and rescued from death after his own disobedience. Now, he was angry because God was kind and showed mercy, since he was not quickly angered. He had great love because he chose not to cause harm.

To be perfectly honest, I've felt the same way Jonah did. I've wanted "justice" to rain down on people I believed had mistreated me. I could almost taste the sweet revenge, and it smacked much more of well-deserved consequences for their bad actions than God's grace and mercy. I wanted things to be "right" (according to me) and for God to ride to my rescue so I could shout at the wrongdoers, *"See! I told you!"*

But God reminds me of something every time I start down this path of defining my own justice—I'm supposed to forgive my enemies and pray blessings for them.

Blessings?

I want to join the Jonah chorus and shout, "No way, God!"

But I also realize choosing forgiveness is for my benefit as well as the other person's. When I forgive, it frees me.

You might be asking, *But what about the praying for blessings part? Surely, I don't have to do that? For those people?*

Yes, and you know what? Praying for our enemies to receive the blessing of salvation works. Salvation is the greatest gift and blessing God can provide, and it's one I can pray for. Looking at a situation God's way is something I can do even if I wanted justice and consequences. In Matthew chapter 5, as part of the Sermon on the Mount, Jesus teaches us to how we are to treat people who mistreat us:

> "You have heard that it was said, 'An eye for an eye, and a tooth for a tooth, but I tell you, don't stand up against an evil person. If someone slaps you on the right cheek, turn to him the other cheek also. If someone wants to sue you in court and take your shirt, let him have your coat also. If someone forces you to go with him one mile, go with him two miles. If a person asks you for something, give it to him. Don't refuse to give to someone who wants to borrow from you. You have heard that it was said, 'Love your neighbor, and hate your enemies.' But I say to you, love your enemies. Pray for those who hurt you. If

you do this, you will be true children of your Father in heaven. He causes the sun to rise on good people and on evil people, and he sends rain to those who do right and to those who do wrong. If you love only the people who love you, you will get no reward. Even the tax collectors do that. And if you are nice only to your friends, you are no better than other people. Even those who don't know God are nice to their friends. So you must be perfect, just as your Father in heaven is perfect. (Matthew 5:38-48)

But how can we be perfect? How can we do these things Jesus is asking of us? We trust if God has told us to do something, he will make it possible. I need only to ask for his help and begin to be obedient. To pray for my enemies and show love for people even while I still want justice and consequences to find their way to the enemy. When I pray in obedience, God will work in my heart.

But how can we be perfect? How can we do these things Jesus is asking of us? We trust if God has told us to do something, he will make it possible. I need only to ask for his help and begin to be obedient. To pray for my enemies and show love for people even while I still want justice and consequences to find their way to the enemy. When I pray in obedience, God will work in my heart. Once my heart is properly focused on him, I will rejoice over the fact that

God is gracious and compassionate, slow to anger, and abounding in love. I remember I need the grace he offers daily and in every moment. And I want others to have it too.

Jonah needed that grace and mercy, and so did the older brother in Jesus' parable. So do we.

It's a testament to God's great love and mercy that he didn't honor Jonah's request. He didn't say to his still-unwilling-prophet, "Okay. You want to die? You got it."

Thankfully God is merciful and forgiving. Like the father who explained to his son the reason for his joy, God wanted Jonah to understand. He started by asking Jonah a question. "Do you think it is right for you to be angry?" (Jonah 4:4)

Drama in the Desert

God's question to Jonah sits there on the page unanswered. Instead of replying, Jonah retreated from the city. Verse 5 tells us, "Jonah went out and sat down east of the city. There he made a shelter for himself and sat in the shade, waiting to see what would happen to the city."

He wanted away from Nineveh, and—I imagine—still hoped those Ninevites were finally going to get what was coming to them.

He waited and watched.

Scripture doesn't record this, but I picture him in his homemade shelter with arms crossed and a scowl on his face. He was not happy, and he wanted to be sure everyone—especially God (who had sent him to this place where he didn't want to come)—knew it.

I know sometimes when I sit and wait there's an internal dialog running. If I'm upset about a particular thing or event, I replay it in my mind. Have you been there? I might picture all I could have done differently or try to form those "perfect" words I could have spoken to possibly get me out of the situation and make others realize just how wrong they'd acted. I imagine Jonah could have had the same kinds of thoughts.

Didn't want to come in the first place.

Better off if I'd drowned or stayed inside that fish.

I tried to tell God to find someone else.

Now look at what's happened.

Of course, God is going to let them off the hook. And they don't even deserve it.

He sat there brooding, hotter than the Assyrian sun shining over his head. And suddenly he noticed it wasn't as hot as it had been. *I must be losing my mind.* Jonah may have squirmed a bit, readjusted his legs and settled back further into the shade. *Does it seem a little cooler around here? Like there's more shade?* Perhaps Jonah finally took his eyes off the city he'd been glowering at and noticed he was now being shaded, not only by the shelter he had thrown together, but by a plant which seemed to grow out of nowhere.

But it wasn't from nowhere.

Verse 6 tells us, "The Lord made a plant grow quickly up over Jonah, which gave him shade and helped him to be more comfortable."

Finally! Something is going my way, Jonah may have thought. I picture him settling back maybe with a small smile on his face (perhaps the first one in quite a while) as he thought about how fortunate he was this plant had grown in exactly the right spot. Maybe he thought, *What a great coincidence!* I wonder how often in my life I have missed God's blessings that way, dismissing them as happenstance and counting myself as lucky.

Verse 6 continues, "Jonah was very pleased to have the plant."

Jonah was so comfortable and happy about this plant, he was able to rest. I imagine he slept, maybe fitfully, but at long last he was starting to feel good about this turn of events. If this were a movie, the lighting would change, and the music would darken. The camera would shift from Jonah's sleeping face to the base of the plant, where the next part of this drama in the desert is about to unfold.

Jonah 4:7 tells us, "But the next day when the sun rose, God sent a worm to attack the plant so that it died."

Maybe Jonah woke to the sun's light dancing across him. I picture him rolling over, hoping to hide his face in the shelter of the plant only to open his eyes and see its withered stalk, its once large leaves shriveled and dead against the parched ground.

Still, Jonah stayed in his shelter, waiting and watching, not knowing things were about to go from bad to worse.

Jonah 4:8 says, "As the sun rose higher in the sky, God sent a very hot east wind to blow, and the sun became so hot on Jonah's head that he became very weak and wished he were dead."

And then Jonah returned to a familiar theme.

The end of verse 8 adds, "He said, 'It is better for me to die than to live.'"

I had one thing going for me—just this plant. That was the only good thing in my whole life, and now it's gone. I'd rather die than go on this way.

In this part of the book, Jonah reminds me of another Old Testament prophet named Elijah. In the book of 1 Kings, we read about God calling Elijah to deliver a message of judgment against a wicked king named Ahab. God told Elijah to pray it wouldn't rain, and the country experienced a drought. In 1 Kings 18:1, we see that God is ready to change things, bringing the long standoff to an end. "During the third year without rain, the Lord spoke his word to Elijah, 'Go and meet King Ahab, and I will soon send rain.'" Elijah sent word to the king, calling for a meeting at a place called Mount Carmel. There, God defeated the prophets of false gods the people were worshipping, sending literal fire from heaven to swallow up the sacrifice Elijah offered on the water-drenched altar. And the prophets who served these false gods were defeated and destroyed (1 Kings 18:16-45). Elijah was triumphant. He received such power from God that he was even able to outrun the chariot of Ahab (1 Kings 18:45).

And then he ran headlong into the wrath of a wicked queen. See, King Ahab went home and told his wife, Jezebel, all the details about what happened on Mount Carmel. Jezebel decided she wasn't done with God's prophet, so she sent Elijah a message saying, "'May the gods punish me terribly if by this time tomorrow I don't kill you just as you killed those prophets" (1 Kings 19:2). She meant to terrify Elijah.

The threat did its job. It scared Elijah and sent him scurrying in fear. He wound up in the wilderness where he settled under a broom bush. (God's prophets seem to like to spend a lot of time under bushes or weeds, but maybe it's just because it was the desert.) Elijah began to pray. His prayer was very different from when he'd powerfully and confidently called on God on top of Mount Carmel.

Here, he was tired and scared. Let's read 1 Kings 19:4-5:

> Then Elijah walked for a whole day into the desert. He sat down under a bush and asked to die. "I have had enough, Lord," he prayed. 'Let me die. I am no better than my ancestors." Then he lay down under the tree and slept.

God saw him there in the shade of the bush and cared for Elijah's hurting heart. He sent an angel to feed him and give him water, not once but twice (1 Kings 19:5-8). Then Elijah traveled further into the wilderness, strengthened by God's nourishment, and was able to keep going for forty days and nights. He went to the mountain of God, Mount Horeb (1 Kings 19:8).

Elijah met with God there, not an angel sent to do his bidding, but the great God of the universe. It's interesting how God came to Elijah this time. On top of Mount Carmel, he'd come in power, but here, in this moment of weakness, he showed a different side to his prophet. There was powerful wind, an earthquake, and a fire, but that wasn't how the Lord came. "After the fire, there was a quiet, gentle sound. When Elijah heard it, he covered his face with his coat and went out and stood at the entrance to the cave" (1 Kings 19:11-13).

A whisper. Quiet. Soft. Easy to miss if we are not paying attention, if we're not close enough to him.

Coming gently like a whisper, God talked with Elijah. He asked him what he was doing there hiding in the mountain cave in the wilderness, and Elijah poured out his heart.

> He answered, "Lord God All-Powerful, I have always served you as well as I could. But the people of Israel have broken their agreement with you, destroyed your altars, and killed your prophets with swords. I am the only prophet left, and now they are trying to kill me too." (1 Kings 19:14)

Don't you know? Don't you care? Those are the questions Elijah's heart cried out as he shared his hurt with the One who could help.

I love the fact God was not angry because Elijah got scared. Unlike how we might react, he did not rage about how wrong it was for Elijah to doubt him. Instead, God gave his prophet two things—

he gave him a new job (both a purpose and a reason to get back to work), and he gave him perspective.

Oh, Elijah. You believe you're the only one who has been faithful to me? Let me tell you the truth...

> "I have seven thousand people left in Israel who have never bowed down before Baal and whose mouths have never kissed his idol." (1 Kings 19:18)

God was not content to leave his prophet Elijah frightened under a bush or defeated in a mountain cave. And God wasn't finished with Jonah either. He met Jonah amid the hot wind under the blazing sun beside the rapidly disappearing remnant of Jonah's surprise plant. And God asked Jonah, "'Do you think it is right for you to be angry about the plant?'" (Jonah 4:9).

Jonah's answer? It's right there at the end of verse 9, "'Is it right for me to be angry? I am so angry I could die!'"

As he did with Elijah, God offered Jonah perspective.

We'll look at the Lord's perspective that he taught Jonah in our next chapter, but sit for a while in the shade, on your comfy chair, or under the sun as hot as when it shone in the Assyrian sky. Think about God's question to Jonah.

"Do you have a right to be angry about the plant?"

Do we have a right to be angry when things don't happen exactly the way we'd planned?

Have you had a metaphorical plant wither on you—one you didn't plant or maybe one you did plant—one you've been angry with God about? A broken relationship? A crushed dream? Financial ruin? A wayward child?

What in your life makes you want to scream at God, "I'd rather die than obey you?"

Tell him about it.

Pour your heart out to God in prayer, dear sister. He can take it, and he will offer you beauty for the ashes of your withered dreams.

What in your life makes you want to scream at God,
"I'd rather die than obey you?" Tell him about it.
Pour your heart out to God in prayer, dear sister.
He can take it, and he will offer you
beauty for the ashes of your withered dreams.

Dive Deeper

Have you ever found yourself in a bad place because of your choices? Have you had thoughts you can never be forgiven? Recognize those thoughts as lies straight out of the pit of hell. 2 Corinthians 5:21 tells us God made Jesus become sin so we might become the righteousness of God.

We can be forgiven.

You can be forgiven.

For anything.

Satan is our very real enemy who will stop at nothing to convince us we are hopeless. He says we are beyond saving.

Know this! He is a liar and a thief and only wants to destroy you. Follow the youngest son's example and return home to the Father.

Like the father in the parable, he is watching for you, ready to forgive and celebrate you.

If you've already found your way home, reflect on who you may know who needs to return to the Father and ask for forgiveness. Ask God to give you the opportunity to talk with them about their spiritual need.

God used a worm to teach his prophet a lesson. Will you examine your own heart? Are you rejoicing about seeing the lost come to Christ, or do you have tendencies to be like the older brother? To be like Jonah?

Journal about what God's grace means to you. Consider how he doesn't give us what we deserve but instead offered his own Son as the payment for our sin and disobedience.

Finally, consider what plant you might be angry with God over? What in your life makes you want to scream at God, "I'd rather die than obey you?"

Prayer of Reflection

Father God, forgive me for my unforgiveness. Help me understand none of us deserves your grace and mercy. Those are beautiful gifts you have given to me and you willingly offer to "whosoever" believes in Jesus as Savior. Give me a heart that rejoices about seeing people come to faith in you. Give me courage to tell others of your great love and mercy so they, too, may be forgiven.

I come to you honestly with my hurts. There are moments and circumstances in my life I just don't understand. Help me with _____. I know the way I feel isn't always right. Lord, help me understand your perspective on my life and my circumstances. I love you, God, and I trust you are good. Show me what I can learn about you. Help me rely on you for my joy and strength. In Jesus' name, amen.

Chapter 9

∽

The Eternal Perspective

(Scripture: Jonah 4:9-11; James 1:22-25)

At the end of our last chapter, we left Jonah angry and irritated beside the withered plant.

I've been there.

Oh, I don't mean I've sat by some dead plant in the actual desert, but I've been hot with rage and mourning over wilted dreams I'd concocted under some misguided idea I could define my own life. I've been absolutely convinced my plans should have worked out the way I'd dreamed.

Wouldn't that relationship have made me so happy?

Can't you just imagine how this perfect opportunity would've changed my life?

God, can't you see how good my plans were?

...I've been hot with rage and mourning over wilted dreams I'd concocted under some misguided idea I could define my own life. I've been absolutely convinced my plans should have worked out the way I'd dreamed.

Jonah sat under the hot sun, and I imagine he wondered something similar. Maybe he asked under his breath or even out loud, *"Didn't God understand those people deserved to be punished? Why does he have to be so forgiving all the time?"*

Unlike Jonah, God didn't get all hot and bothered. He met Jonah beside the remains of the withered plant and shared his heart.

> "And the Lord said, 'You are so concerned about the plant even though you did nothing to make it grow. It appeared one day, and the next day it died'" (Jonah 4:10)

God wanted Jonah to zero in on why he was upset. He wanted Jonah to realize he really didn't have a right to be angry because this plant had died. "Jonah," he is saying, "You didn't even plant this seed. It just sprang up and is now gone. It wasn't yours Jonah; it never was."

Then God shifted the focus back to the people of Nineveh, who have almost been forgotten in the drama over the plant. Forgotten by the reader, and maybe for a few moments by Jonah, but never by God.

John 4:8 tells us "God is love." That truth is on full display as God asked Jonah another question,

> "Then shouldn't I show concern for the great city of Nineveh, which has more than 120,000 people who do not know right from wrong, and many animals, too?" (Jonah 4:11)

The translation I quoted says the 120,000 do not know right from wrong; others say they don't know "right from left." Some scholars think this could mean there were 120,000 children under two years old—too young to know right from left—inside Nineveh. If this only refers to small children, think how many people this would mean lived in the capital.

God wanted Jonah to think about them as people and not just "the great city of Nineveh." Along the streets and inside homes and businesses of this city were thousands of individuals. Each was a person God had created in his own image. Men, women, and children he knew and cared about deeply. God knew them all by name; he even knew how many hairs were on their heads. Thousands and thousands of people.

I am thankful God is not as sarcastic as I can be. I'd want to yell at Jonah, "All these people you'd want to wipe off the face of the earth without a second thought. No, you don't want to do it—you want me, the God who loves, to do it. And the only thing you see wrong here is a plant which grew in the desert wound up withered. Is the dead plant really all you see wrong, Jonah? Really?"

God was helping Jonah see, and through the pages of Scripture helps us understand his care and concern for people. "Shouldn't I show concern?" he asked in Jonah 4:11. He wanted to draw the people of Nineveh to him and would relent on his punishment if they were willing to respond. He will do the same for us.

God was helping Jonah to see, and through the pages of Scripture helps us understand his care and concern for people. "Shouldn't I show concern?" he asked in Jonah 4:11. He wanted to draw the people of Nineveh to him and would relent on his punishment if they were willing to respond. He will do the same for us.

Hebrews 13:8 tells us Jesus Christ is "the same yesterday, today and forever." This is an attribute of God. Back in Genesis 16:13, a woman named Hagar called God "the God who sees me." She was in distress, had been mistreated and abused, cast aside and nearly forgotten. But God saw her. He cared.

Job called God "you watcher of humans" (Job 7:20), and the psalmist wrote, "From his throne he watches all who live on earth" (Psalm 33:14).

Jesus explained this point: "Two sparrows cost only a penny, but not even one of them can die without your Father's knowing it. God even knows how many hairs are on your head. So don't be afraid. You are worth much more than many sparrows" (Matthew 10:29-31).

Jesus could have said those words to the people of Nineveh. They were worth more than many sparrows. He saw what happened to them. He cared. It's why he sent his less-than-willing, far-from-perfect prophet to preach to them. He wanted them to repent. He wanted to draw the people to himself. He loved them.

Because God is love. The apostle John tells us so in 1 John 4:8,

"Whoever does not love does not know God, because God is love."

As people who have the New Testament teachings, we can know this is God's plan for us and has been part of God's plan all along. Jesus often taught about the importance of us showing love.

"I give you a new command: Love each other. You must love each other as I have loved you" (John 13:34).

"Jesus answered, 'Love the Lord your God with all your heart, all your soul, and all your mind. This is the first and most important command. And the second command is like the first: Love your neighbor as you love yourself'" (Matthew 22:37-39).

At this point in Jonah I always flip to the next page, ready to read Chapter 5 and find out how Jonah responded, how God used him throughout the rest of his life. But the book of Jonah ends with God's question to Jonah.

I remember reading stories in middle and high school English classes that ended with a sentence in bold print and capital letters: "write the rest of the story." I sometimes think Jonah should end this way. After all, it is up to us to write the rest of our own story.

We must decide if we will be part of reaching the Ninevites of our world, or if we will sit by the remains of a wilted plant with our arms crossed mad at the world and mad at God, wishing we could just die.

We must decide if we will be part of reaching the Ninevites of our world, or if we will sit by the remains of a wilted plant with our arms crossed mad at the world and mad at God, wishing we could just die.

Lessons Learned

We have wandered a long way with Jonah. We have watched as he received the call, fled, got swallowed by a fish, repented, was spit up, and finally obeyed. We've heard him tell God—in words and actions—that he'd rather die than obey. We have seen him angry because God didn't mete out justice according to "the Jonah scale." Jonah has been fuming mad over the way God forgave the people of Nineveh, and he was more concerned about a worm causing "his" plant to wilt than he was the hearts of others.

Along the way, we have also gotten to know a lot about God. This tiny book in Scripture has revealed how God cared for the Ninevites and why he offers second chances—to Jonah, to Nineveh, and to us. We've listened to his heart as he shared with Jonah. Now, it's time to decide what we will do with all of this knowledge we've accumulated.

Does God Understand?

Jonah was asked to do a hard thing: to be God's messenger to his enemies. Reading about his experiences may make us wonder if God would really ask him to take a message of redemption to difficult people? Well, that's exactly what happened.

And that's precisely what God calls us to do as well. To love, even in difficult circumstances. To shine the light of his salvation into the darkness, perhaps even among the very last people we would want to share it with.

And that's precisely what God calls us to do as well. To love, even in difficult circumstances. To shine the light of his salvation into the darkness, perhaps even among the very last people we would want to share it with.

It was too much for Jonah. He tried to run away from God, to separate himself from this overwhelming call. He cried out to God numerous times with a clear response, "Let me die."

Basically, his heart's cry was *"I'd rather die than obey."*

Jonah's encounter raises important questions:

Will we respond differently than he did?

Will we be obedient, even when it hurts?

How can God ask us to do difficult things?

Why would he do it?

Doesn't he understand?

Questions like these echo through our hearts even as Satan uses our pain and hurts to tell us to forget following God and just run as far away as possible.

That plan didn't work for Jonah, and it will not work for us.

Let's take a few moments to review four major themes we've discussed: God's omnipresence, God's love, obedience, and our own judgmental hearts. Let's see how these help us know how to move forward into the abundant life available to us as sons and daughters of God.

God's Omnipresence. When Jonah chose to disobey God's call to go to Nineveh, he found out firsthand there was nowhere he could go to outrun God's presence. Jonah began to run away to Tarshish (practically the end of the known world in his day), but even that distant place would not have been far enough away to escape God. Heading down into the depths of the sea was not deep enough. God was still there.

Rather than feeling fearful, we can rejoice with the psalmist and find comfort knowing there is nowhere we can go where God will not be. There is no situation in which God won't take care of us. There is no problem he can't solve and no pain he can't understand as he carries us through. Oh dear sister, I've found this so true in difficult, troubling seasons, and I encourage you to cultivate a practice of thanking God for his constant presence wherever you find yourself today or in all the tomorrows to come.

My prayer is you will not leave these pages without finding the forgiveness, grace, and mercy Jesus offers. I also pray we Christian women will remember the price he paid for our sins and live in light of the victory he offers. Let's reflect his love and joy through all our moments and all our days.

God's Love. The book of Jonah paints a very clear picture of the heart of God. He loved the sinful people of Nineveh. He loves sinful people like me and you.

The Bible teaches that sin entered the human story and separated us from the Holy God. Nothing we could ever do would be enough to earn our way back into a restored relationship with him. We were completely hopeless. But God loved us so much he sent his Son Jesus to die for us so we would not have to pay the penalty for our sins.

We could not have made up for our sinfulness even if we had wanted to. Jesus became a willing sacrifice who died in our place and was resurrected to claim victory over death. Now, we can accept Jesus as our Savior by receiving the gift he offers. And we get everlasting life in the mix.

My prayer is you will not leave these pages without finding the forgiveness, grace, and mercy Jesus offers. I also pray we Christian women will remember the price he paid for our sins and live in light of the victory he offers. Let's reflect his love and joy through all our moments and all our days.

Obedience. God invites us into his family. He gives us assignments and sends us as his messengers to people. But we, like Jonah, have a choice. Will we obey or will we go running to the ends of the earth to get away from God's call?

I saw a quote on social media the other day that contained humorous, but sage advice. "Learn from the mistakes of others. You can't live long enough to make them all yourself." [33] This is part of the beauty of having books like Jonah in Scripture. We can learn from Jonah's disobedience without making the same mistake ourselves.

By reading of Jonah's life, we see our disobedience can land us in all kinds of trouble, whether we wind up swallowed by a great fish or not. When we are willfully outside of God's plan for our lives, we often feel miserable. Unfulfilled. Discontent. It may lead us to complete and utter despair. God wants better for our lives.

By reading of Jonah's life, we see our disobedience can land us in all kinds of trouble, whether we wind up swallowed by a great fish or not. When we are willfully outside of God's plan for our lives, we often feel miserable. Unfulfilled. Discontent. It may lead us to complete and utter despair.

God wants better for our lives.

He invites us into deeper relationship with him, and when we are obedient, he promises to give us peace beyond understanding. He offers rest, and when we are in a healthy relationship with him, he gives us true contentment.

Remember, we obey God not because we are fearful of consequences, but because it shows our love for him.

Obedience often feels hard because the Enemy tells us it will be difficult. He whispers lies like, *"God won't really take care of you. You'd be better off dead than listening to and obeying God."* When we think things like "I'd rather die than obey," we are falling for the trap Satan has been using for thousands of years. He wants us to not trust God. But Jonah's life helps us see how perfectly trustworthy God is and that he acts out of his great love, even when we don't understand what we're being asked to do.

*Jonah's life helps us see how perfectly trustworthy God is
and that he acts out of his great love, even when we don't
understand what we're being asked to do.*

Let's be women who embrace obedience completely, who jump
up when we first feel God calling. I pray we will pursue closeness
with God with all our hearts, minds, and souls.

Our Judgmental Hearts. Once we have accepted Jesus as our
Savior, we face the new challenge of recognizing and remembering
we are no more deserving of his love than people around us, then
live in light of that truth. None of us are righteous. Jesus is the
righteous one; we can be forgiven only when covered by his blood.
Once we accept him as Savior, we must be careful to guard against
thinking too highly of ourselves. The New Testament is full of
examples of religious people who thought they were better than
others. Any righteousness we have is only because of Jesus Christ!

I pray we will remember this truth every day. We can thank Jesus
for paying the price for our sins regularly and ask God to give us eyes
to see the people around us the way he does—as individuals created
in his image and in need of the same mercy and grace we've received.
The world does its best to divide us, to convince us to see others as
different, or even as enemies. Satan will use our hurts against us.

Let's confess our judgmental hearts and view our world with the
loving eyes of our heavenly Father. May He guide us to be women
who share his love with our world, both when our circle includes
our friends and family members and when it includes people we may
be tempted to think are not worthy of grace and mercy. It doesn't
matter whether you remember how Jonah thought of the Ninevites,
but please always remember how God thought about them and why.

(Spoiler alert! None of us are worthy of grace and mercy. This is what makes them such amazing gifts from God.)

As we turn the final pages of this book, drop it onto our table, or tuck it away on our electronic bookshelf, I hope we will not forget about Jonah and how we can choose to write our own life story.

Jesus' half-brother James wrote,

> Do what God's teaching says: when you only listen and do nothing, you are fooling yourselves. Those who hear God's teaching and do nothing are like people who look at themselves in a mirror. They see their faces and then go away and quickly forget what they looked like. But the truly happy people are those who carefully study God's perfect law that makes people free, and they continue to study it. They do not forget what they heard, but they obey what God's teaching says. Those who do this will be made happy. (James 1:22-25)

My words are unimportant. I pray anything I have written that may be unnecessary will fall away. But the Word of God captured in the book of Jonah is living and breathing and has so much to teach us, even a few millennia after Jonah sat under the blistering Assyrian sun.

Perhaps the prophet Isaiah said it best. "The grass dies and the flowers fall, but the Word of our God will live forever" (Isaiah 40:8).

God is calling us, first to repentance and salvation, then he is sending us on a mission. We have two choices: to tell God "I'd rather die than obey," or to say "I trust you, Lord, and know you are good; I will obey you whatever the cost." How will you answer his call?

God is calling us, first to repentance and salvation, then he is sending us on a mission.

We have two choices: to tell God "I'd rather die than obey," or to say "I trust you, Lord, and know you are good; I will obey you whatever the cost."

How will you answer his call?

Dive Deeper

Sit for a few moments and ask God to show you what he would like to change about the next chapter of your story. As you prepare to leave Jonah by the remains of the plant, how will you go forward? Write what God is telling you.

As we leave behind our study of the book of Jonah, reflect on what God has taught you through his prophet. How will you respond because of this once-stinky prophet and the account between him,

Nineveh, and the God who loves everyone?

Prayer of Reflection

Dear Lord, thank you for the truth of your Scripture. I ask you to change me because of the time I have spent with Jonah. Help us leave these pages different than when we started, changed because we have encountered you. Help us to examine ourselves and to invite you to examine our hearts. Show us where we need to confess our sins. Teach us to see our world and all the people in it through your eyes. Teach us to carry word of your great love and your offer of forgiveness to any and all who would hear it. Along the way we will be careful to give you all the glory and honor. In the precious name of Jesus, we pray.

Amen and amen.

For Additional Study

～

Recommendations
for Group Study

Dear Sister in Christ,

Thank you for your interest in sharing this study reflecting on the book of Jonah with other women. The following recommendations for group study are offered to aid you in preparing to lead your group.

Each week begins with a list of readings to be completed by the leader and participants before the meeting. Encourage participants to bring a print or digital copy of the Bible with them to class each week so they can look up the Scriptures studied.

The questions included in the outline are intended to encourage your thinking and are not designed as a strict formula to be followed. Depending on the amount of discussion and the size of your group, you may only be able to include a few of the questions in each session. Remember not all participants will be at the same point in their faith journey. The book includes tools to help you guide women to salvation in Christ. Don't skip over them too quickly in your sessions, but also seek opportunities to discuss this topic with each woman individually. Encourage group members to talk with you or someone else if they have made a decision for Christ or would like more information on how to do so.

My prayer is you will enjoy the unique perspective your group brings to this study and allow the Holy Spirit to lead you.

In Christ's Love,

Dawn Tolbert

Week 1 Study Outline

Before the group time:
Read the book of Jonah and chapters 1 and 2 of this book

Begin your time together in prayer asking the Holy Spirit to guide your study and open everyone's heart to his teaching.

Questions for Discussion

Where are you on the "Jonah Journey"? Is the book familiar or are you discovering it for the first time? Is Jonah simply a Bible story remembered from childhood that you haven't thought much about since?

In Chapter 1, the author shared her Jonah story about struggling to write this book. Have you had an experience where you felt called to do something but were reluctant to do so because of fear or not feeling adequate to the task? Or maybe like Jonah you didn't like God's plan? What did you learn from that experience? What drew you back to the Lord?

The author wrote: "(In our study of Jonah,) we will see how we can trust God, even with our angry, hurt, or unforgiving thoughts as we draw near to him. Lean into those questions. Ask God the things that keep you awake at night, then listen for his answer." Have you asked God hard questions? What can you share about that experience?

Reflect on the meaning of Jonah's name discussed in Chapter 2. What insights did you learn about Jonah's mission from studying his name? What does this teach us about God?

Why do you think Jonah disliked the Ninevites so much?

How would you respond if you were asked to share God's forgiveness with people who completely disagree with your way of life or who have hurt you in some way?

The author wrote, "Obedience is a gift we give to God because he is worthy of our trust, our faith, and our actions to accomplish what he has asked of us. We choose to obey because it honors him." Do you agree or disagree? Why?

Make a list of practical steps we can take toward obedience.

How would you define the word covenant? Can you think of modern-day examples?

Why do you think God establishes covenants? With Abraham? With Israel? With us?

How should being part of a covenant relationship change our behavior?

God loves us (and he loved the Ninevites) despite our sinful nature. What does that mean to you?

Closing Prayer

Dear heavenly Father, thank you for the peace and truth you offer to us. Lord, help us live in light of the difference you have made in us through your Son Jesus. Help us to be willing to go to others to tell them about your goodness and your grace. In Jesus' name, amen.

Week 2 Study Outline

Before the group time:
Read Jonah 1-2 and chapters 3-4 of this book.

Begin your time together in prayer asking the Holy Spirit to guide your study and open everyone's heart to his teaching.

Questions for Discussion

In your own words, describe how far Jonah was willing to go to get away from God. How do you think Jonah may have felt as he was running away?

Would anyone like to share about a time when God asked you to do something and you said no or were reluctant to say yes? Did you eventually say yes? What did you learn about God through that experience?

Jonah went a long way to disobey God. How far are we willing to go to obey God?

How does Abraham's obedience to God in Genesis 12 contrast with what we know of Jonah's story so far?

How would you have felt if you had been in Corrie Ten Boom's situation? What would it have felt like to be asked to forgive someone who treated you and your loved ones so horribly? Why does God ask us to do such hard things?

Have you ever tried to delay obedience or to get out of obeying completely? What did God teach you through that experience?

The psalmist David viewed God's omnipresence—the knowledge there's no place we can go where he won't be—as a blessing. How does the knowledge God is everywhere make you feel?

Is your response to the last question more like David's or Jonah's? Why do you think that is the case?

James 4:8 tells us if we come near to God, he will come near to us. What are some tangible things you can do this week to draw near to God?

Closing Prayer

Dear Sovereign Lord, our minds cannot fully grasp your omnipresence and your sovereignty. We know your thoughts are higher than our thoughts, and we submit to you. Thank you for giving us second chances when we have disobeyed you.

Help us to trust you, obey you, fear you, and honor you as the one true God. Thank you for loving us. Help us to live each day with a renewed appreciation of what it means to be your daughters. In Jesus' name we pray, amen.

Week 3 Study Outline

Before the group time:
Read Jonah 1-2 and chapter 5 of this book.

Begin your time together in prayer asking the Holy Spirit to guide your study and open everyone's heart to his teaching.

Questions for Discussion

One theme of the book of Jonah is "God is more powerful than our plans." What did this look like for Jonah?

How have you experienced this truth in your own life or seen it in other Scriptures?

As we near the end of chapter 1 of Jonah, we read the pagan sailors' reaction after Jonah was thrown overboard. Scripture says they "began to fear the Lord very much." What do you think "fearing the Lord" may have meant for them? Why were they hesitant to throw Jonah overboard?

What does "fearing the Lord" look like in our lives? Does that mean God wants us quaking in our boots, or do you think scripture is pointing us to something different?

Briefly review the encounter between Jonah and the sailors as the storm was raging. How do you think Jonah must have felt as he realized the sailors were going to throw him overboard and he found himself falling into the water?

Have you ever faced a time where you felt you received what you deserved because of your actions? What did you learn about God through the experience?

Read Lamentations 3:22-24 in two or more translations. What does it mean to you to know God's mercies are new every morning? Does this truth help us? How?

Read Jonah's prayer in Jonah 2:2-8. What words or phrases stood out most to you from this passage? Jonah moves from despair to hope to praise. How can we follow his example when we face difficulties of our own?

Jonah praised God and thanked him for salvation while still inside the great fish. He spoke of being delivered before the fish coughed him up on land. Likewise, the author shared how God comforted her during her breast cancer diagnosis. When have you felt God's presence with you while you were still in the middle of dark and desperate circumstances?

How does responding with praise help in difficult times? What are tangible ways we can remind ourselves to take our eyes off our problems and focus on God?

God does not always deliver us from our dark circumstances quickly. In fact, deliverance may not come in this life at all. Relationships may never be restored; deliverance may not come as we hope; and healing may not happen this side of eternity. In chapter 5, the author shared about watching her brother praise God while dying of pancreatic cancer. He died less than six months after receiving his diagnosis but was still able to praise God through the circumstances. How is it possible for us to still have hope and faith even if deliverance does not come?

Closing Prayer

Dear heavenly Father, we know you are good and trustworthy. We praise you, even in the middle of difficult days, seasons, or circumstances. Thank you for the hope and joy you offer to us even when the world would tell us it does not make sense to believe. Help us fix our eyes on Jesus, our eternal hope. In his precious name we pray, amen.

ॐ

Week 4 Study Outline

Before the group time:
Read Jonah 3 and chapter 6 of this book

Begin your time together in prayer asking the Holy Spirit to guide your study and open everyone's heart to his teaching.

Questions for Discussion

Chapter 6 of this book begins with a discussion of "foxhole moments" or times when people find themselves in difficult circumstances and promise God they will change. List examples of this type of promise either from personal experience or from TV shows, movies or books.

Why do you think people make promises like this to God when they face hard times? Why may those promises be difficult to keep once the crisis is over?

Once Jonah was standing on dry ground, he faced another choice: would he obey God and go to Nineveh or would he try running away again? The author wrote, "The Ninevites haven't changed. The animosity between the Ninevites and the people of Israel hasn't changed. The question is: has Jonah changed?" Do you think Jonah had truly changed after his experience inside the fish? What do Jonah's actions tell us?

What do you think of the following statements: "Growth is a process. We may be ready to take the next step of obedience but may still need to grow in our relationship with and trust of God. Jonah still had some growing to do, and so do we." Do you agree or disagree? Why?

Read 1 John 1:9, Psalm 103:12, and Hebrews 8:12. What do these verses teach you about God's offer of forgiveness? What does this mean to you personally at this point in your life? How have they helped you grow as a Christ-follower or how do you think they might help you grow in the future?

One section of this book is titled "Considering the Inconsiderable." Have you ever felt small and unimportant? Have you felt this way when it came to something you thought God was calling you to do? If so, what truths from God's Word helped you when facing this fear?

What does the fact that God uses people from places like Jonah's small hometown mean to you? What about God's willingness to use imperfect people like Jonah, like the author, and like all of us? What can we learn about God from reflecting on these points?

Closing Prayer

Dear heavenly Father, thank you for including us in your work. We know we have no credentials of our own to make us worthy. In fact, we could not be more unworthy. But in your grace and mercy, you choose us. Thank you for this truth! May we always celebrate the fact it is you through Jesus Christ who make us worthy. Praise the Lord! In Jesus' name, amen.

Week 5 Study Outline

Before the group time:
Read Jonah 3 and chapter 7 of this book

Begin your time together in prayer asking the Holy Spirit to guide your study and open everyone's heart to his teaching.

Questions for Discussion

The author mentions the film *Jesus Revolution* and shares how a main character, Greg, struggled to put his faith in Jesus. He asked, "What if it's just another empty high that fades?" What things do people put their faith in other than God?

Read Jonah 3:5-10. What steps did the Ninevites take to show they were sorry for their sin?

Toward the end of this passage, the king says, "Who knows? Maybe God will change his mind. Maybe he will stop being angry, and then we will not die." Is the king sure they will be saved by repenting?

Read 1 John 1:9, Acts 3:18, Hebrews 10:17, and Ephesians 1:7. How do these verses show the salvation offered through Jesus Christ contrasts with the Ninevite king's "maybe God will change his mind" statement?

What does it mean to you to be offered adoption into God's family? To be considered a beloved child rather than an outsider worthy of judgment?

Near the end of the chapter, the author wrote, "God is holy. Perfect. Just. We are not. We are sinful people who are unable to live up to God's standards for our life. His standard is holiness. Perfection. Without spiritual blemish. Absolutely just and righteous. Do those descriptions sound like you? Well, it didn't sound like me either." Why are we unable to live up to God's standards on our own?

What does it mean to you that Jesus came to bridge the gap between us as sinful people and the holy, perfect God? Using the A-B-Cs of faith included in this chapter, explain what we need to do to receive God's free gift of salvation.

Would you like to pray to receive salvation? Use the prayer included in chapter 7 of the book, and be sure to talk with your group leader and/or other study participants about your decision.

Closing Prayer

Dear sovereign Lord, thank you for grace and mercy and forgiveness while we were still sinners. Help us know your saving power can transform any life because we know the miracle it took to transform our own. We praise you and thank you for Jesus in whose name we pray. Amen.

Week 6 Study Outline

Before the group time:
Read Jonah 4 and chapters 8-9 of this book

Begin your time together in prayer asking the Holy Spirit to guide your study and open everyone's heart to his teaching.

Questions for Discussion

The lost son in Jesus' third parable made terrible decisions and wound up wishing he could eat the food meant for pigs. Have you ever found yourself in a bad place because of your choices? Have you heard thoughts saying you can never be forgiven? Consider how those might have been lies Satan used to keep us separated from God.

Read 2 Corinthians 5:21. What does it mean for us to become "the righteousness of God"? What makes us clean? Is it something we can do for ourselves?

Read Luke 15:25-32. Why do you think the older brother was not happy about his younger brother's return home?

Read Jonah 4:1-4. Jonah tells God, "I knew that you are a God who is kind and shows mercy. You don't become angry quickly, and you have great love. I knew you would choose to not cause harm" (Jonah 4:2). Jonah seems to be accusing God with this statement. What do you think of Jonah's attitude considering his past?

Prayerfully consider the following: Are you rejoicing over seeing the lost come to Christ, or do you have tendencies to be like the older brother? To be like Jonah? Why might this be a hard thing for us to do?

What does God's grace and mercy mean to you personally? What do they mean for others?

Read Jonah 4:4-9. God asked Jonah, "Do you have a right to be angry about the plant?" Do we have a right to be angry with God when things don't happen exactly the way we'd planned?

Have you had a metaphorical plant wither on you—one you didn't plant or maybe even one you did plant—and you've been angry with God about it? A broken relationship? A crushed dream? Financial ruin? A wayward child?

How have you experienced God offering beauty for the ashes of your withered dreams in these circumstances? How will you look for that beauty in the future?

The author introduces the story of the prophet Elijah. We see him not always in great victory, but tired and depressed and utterly convinced he is alone in his service to God. God saw Elijah in the shade of the bush and gave him food, a new purpose, and a fresh, true vision. How has God restored you in seasons of depression and despair?

Read Jonah 4:9-11. What did God want Jonah to understand about the plant? What was God trying to teach Jonah about how he saw the people of Nineveh?

1 John 4:8 tells us God is love. What impact does the fact "God is love" have on our lives and how we interact with others?

As the book of Jonah draws to a close, God asks, "Then shouldn't I show concern for the great city of Nineveh, which has more than one hundred twenty thousand people who do not know right from wrong, and many animals too" (Jonah 4:11). The author says she always wants to turn the page to find Chapter 5 to see how Jonah responded. But our encounter with Jonah ends with the question. She adds, "We get to decide if we will be part of reaching the Ninevites of our world, or if we are just going to sit by the remains of a wilted plant with our arms crossed, mad at the world and mad at God, wishing we could just die." What do you sense God would like you to change about the next chapter of your story?

How will you choose to go forward different because of this time in God's Word?

In the final chapter of this book, the author points out four key topics we have learned about from our study of Jonah: God's Omnipresence, God's Love, Obedience, and Our Judgmental Hearts. Which of these topics spoke to you most during this study? Why?

What practical steps can you take to live differently because of this study? James 1:22 tells us we should do what God's Word says rather than letting it go in one ear and out the other. Because of your time studying Jonah, how do you plan to be more of a do-er of the Word and not just a hearer?

Closing Prayer

Dear Holy God, thank you for the gift of the women who have been on this journey together with us. Lord, make us more like you because we have spent time studying your Word. Help us to be more like Jesus as we go. We love you. Help us to love others well in your name. We ask all this in the powerful name of Jesus. Amen.

References

1. Scripture quotations marked (NLT) are taken from the Holy Bible, New Living Translation, copyright ©1996, 2004, 2015 by Tyndale House Foundation. Used by permission of Tyndale House Publishers, Carol Stream, Illinois 60188. All rights reserved.

2. https://bibleproject.com/explore/video/jonah/

3. Sproul, R. The Holiness of God. Revised Edition, Tyndale Momentum, 2000.

4. Hayford, J.W., Ed. The New Spirit-Filled Life Bible. 2014. Thomas Nelson, Word Wealth: Entry for "Prophet," p. 339.

5. Smith's Bible Dictionary (1994). Revised Edition. Nashville, Tenn.: Holman Bible Publishers.

6. https://literarydevices.net/symbolism/

7. http://www.biblestudytools.com/commentaries/matthew-henry-complete/jonah/1.html

8. Verrett, Bethany. "What do doves symbolize in the Bible." https://www.biblestudytools. com/bible-study/topical-studies/what-do-doves-symbolize-in-the-bible.html.

9. https://www.behindthename.com/name/amittai

10. https://www.britannica.com/topic/Book-of-Jonah retrieved 11/14/2022

11. Butler, Trent C. Editor. Entry for 'Covenant'. Holman Bible Dictionary. https://www.studylight.org/dictionaries/eng/hbd/c/covenant.html. 1991.

12. http://www.biblestudytools.com/dictionaries/smiths-bible-dictionary/nineveh.html

13. https://www.bibleodyssey.org/en/places/related-articles/nineveh-as-sin-city

14. http://www.biblestudytools.com/commentaries/matthew-henry-complete/jonah/1.html

15. Packer, J I. *Knowing God.* London: Hodder and Stoughton, 1975. Print.

16. https://www.gotquestions.org/Jonah-Tarshish-Nineveh.html

17. Smith, Charles Ward. "Commentary on Jonah 1:4". "Smith's Bible Commentary". https://www.studylight.org/commentaries/csc/jonah-1.html. 2014.

18. Ibid.

19. Charles Haddon Spurgeon, Sermon, "The Obedience of Faith" preached August 21, 1890; retrieved from https://www.spurgeon.org/resource-library/sermons/the-obedience-of-faith/#flipbook/

20. Boom, C., Sherrill, J., & Sherrill, E. (1920). *The Hiding Place.* Bantam.

21. International Standard Bible Encyclopedia, Entry for Omnipresent, biblestudytools.com/dictionary/omnipresence/

22. Tozer, A.W. *The Knowledge of the Holy.* Cambridge: The Lutterworth Press, 1961. Print.

23. http://languages.oup.com/google-dictionary-en.html: precious

24. Lucado, M., editor. *The Devotional Bible: Experiencing the Heart of Jesus.* 1991. Thomas Nelson Bibles.

25. http://www.basicknowledge101.com/subjects/brain.html

26. https://www.technologyreview.com/s/415041/new-measure-of-human-brain-processing-speed/

27. http://biblehub.com/topical/g/gath-hepher.htm

28. http://www.dictionary.com/browse/inconsiderable

29. http://www.dictionary.com/browse/vast

30. Jesus Revolution. Erwin, J. and McCorkle, B. Lionsgate, 2023.

31. Packer, J I. *Knowing God.* London: Hodder and Stoughton, 1975. Print.

32. Scripture quotations marked (NIV) are taken from the Holy Bible, NEW INTERNATIONAL VERSION®, NIV® Copyright © 1973, 1978, 1984, 2011 by Biblica, Inc.® Used by permission. All rights reserved worldwide.

33. http://www.quotationspage.com/quote/38694.html

Acknowledgements

This book has been years in the making.

The first draft of the manuscript was written almost a decade before publication, but the seeds were planted while I was just a small girl. They have been growing for a lifetime, and I pray they will continue to bear fruit long after I am gone.

I am truly grateful to my parents, Jimmy and Barbara Camp, for raising my sister, brother, and me in a Christian home and introducing us to the truth of God's Word from an early age. They taught us what it means to walk with Christ daily.

Little of my writing would be possible without the support of my husband Larry, who gives me room to spread my wings even when the attempt is time consuming and difficult.

I am grateful for my people:

- my big sister Beth Dorsey and big brother Nathan Camp who were my first friends and make (and have made) my world a much better place;
- for Alan Storey and Shannon Biggers who helped raise me professionally and became more like family than coworkers;
- for Dana Thompson, who listens to my wild ideas and dreams alongside me;
- for writer friends Kristen Terrette and Jennifer Henn who encouraged at times and pushed at others, always just on time;
- for Debbie Moon and Debbie Rasure, who pray for me and share sweet friendship;
- For beta readers and Bible study buddies Sarah Lancaster and Zella Musick.

I also am grateful to all the individuals who sacrificially served through the local church to teach, lead music, or encourage. These faith-filled believers have made an indelible mark on my life. Among them are generations of women who chose to love and serve. I pray I will walk faithfully in the footsteps that sought to follow Jesus and to teach others to do so.

Just a few weeks before publication I learned of the passing of Dr. Bill Stowe, my major professor and newspaper advisor during my undergraduate years. His lectures walked me through the Norman Invasion and birth of the English language, into the deep waters of Milton's *Paradise Lost,* and onward to begin to plumb the depths of communication theory. He taught me new ways to love the Lord with my mind as well as my heart and actions. Always, always he required excellence and depth of thought.

I am also grateful for the influence on my education of Dr. Joyce Brown, who taught English and served as advisor to our literary magazine. She encouraged me to strengthen the poetry in my prose and taught me to find beauty in the stories of the people of Appalachia. She helped hone my love of language while expanding my view of the world and, most importantly, the people we share it with.

I thank my editor Nina Hundley, the great folks at the Alliance of Independent Authors, and my CPA friend Britt Madden Jr., all of whom offered great advice and encouragement for this writing and publishing journey. I am forever grateful and will leave you with one piece of advice I received along the path:

Just a few more steps to see what God will do.

Steady on.

Let's walk forward in bold obedience because Jesus is so incredibly worthy of our devotion.

∽

About the Author

Dawn Tolbert is an author who loves to encourage frazzled women on their faith journey. A Bible study teacher for nearly three decades, she taught preschoolers, upper elementary students, and high schoolers before settling in to teach women. She has led missions groups for women and is an active volunteer at her church, singing in the choir and serving as a buddy for special needs adults.

Life is hectic for this 50-something-year-old career woman. Goal-oriented and apparently convinced eventually she will find the perfect planner that will help her hold everything together, Dawn can easily find herself slipping into the habit of striving in her own power. She needs regular reminders to be still and turn her focus to God. So, she writes to help herself (and her readers) remember to break free from that vicious cycle and unwrap God's gift of rest!

Beginning her career as a journalist working for her hometown newspaper, she established a regular series of features to celebrate community life. She was promoted to city editor before earning a spot as features writer and then editor for the lifestyle section at the daily newspaper in a neighboring city. Dawn's writing talents drew the attention of the head of public relations at a nearby college, and she was hired as the college's PR writer. Serving as editor of the college's alumni publication, she played an instrumental role in the creation of the college's alumni magazine.

During her more than 28-year career in higher education public relations, the award-winning communications professional has written for a variety of publications and led key projects including the inaugurations of two college presidents. She currently writes for the Advancement department at Berry College.

Dawn holds a Bachelor of Arts with majors in Communication Studies and English from Gardner-Webb University (North Carolina), a Master of Arts in Professional Writing from Kennesaw State University (Georgia), and a Doctor of Education in Higher Education Leadership from Union University (Tennessee).

At DawnTolbert.com and through her podcast, *Unwrapping Rest with Dawn Tolbert*, she shares what God is teaching her in the difficult, beautiful, and mundane moments of life, praying readers will find encouragement that helps us all shine brighter for the Lord. Dawn was a contributing writer for *Drawing Near*, a collection of devotionals produced by Wholly Loved Ministries. Her devotions have also appeared on Crosswalk. She and husband Larry make their home in Northwest Georgia.

Join the mailing list at
DawnTolbert.com
& be among the first to know
about upcoming books

❧   ❧   ❧   ❧   ❧

EilaImpressions.com

SHOP ONLINE TODAY

Discover more hope-filled, faith-building encouragement

www.ingramcontent.com/pod-product-compliance
Lightning Source LLC
Chambersburg PA
CBHW070702130626
46553CB00005B/1805